The Essential Guide to...

CHILDREN & SEPARATION

SURVIVING DIVORCE & FAMILY BREAK-UP

Dedication

To all the people who have trusted me with their stories.

The Essential Guide to...

CHILDREN & SEPARATION
SURVIVING DIVORCE & FAMILY BREAK-UP

Jennifer Croly

LION

Published by Lion Books
an imprint of
Lion Hudson plc
Wilkinson House, Jordan Hill Road,
Oxford OX2 8DR, England
www.lionhudson.com/lion

ISBN 978 0 7459 55896
e-ISBN 978 0 7459 57692

First edition 2013

A catalogue record for this book is available from the British Library

Printed and bound in the UK, July 2013, LH26

Contents

Introduction

More than one in four children will experience parental divorce by age sixteen (Joseph Rowntree Foundation – www.jrf.org.uk). As I write, our legal and political leaders are discussing a review of the divorce laws in Britain, conscious that many children are hurting but disagreeing about the best way to help make the divorce process easier. In truth even the most amicable divorce is painful, and the most long drawn-out and contested can be damaging for all involved. And very much involved but largely powerless are the children of the marriage.

This book is about how to help or support children whose parents are divorcing. If you are looking for a book to help yourself or friends who are divorcing, then I can only tell you what helped me, and that is written in my first book, *Missing Being Mrs*.[1] If you want help with the legal side of divorce, go to www.sfla.co.uk, which puts it all very simply. If you are a parent, grandparent, friend, teacher, youth worker or pastor of children whose parents are separated, and you're concerned for what the children want and how you could help them, then this book's for you.

Every child reacts differently to their parents separating, but the good news is that statistics show that the majority of children grow up to be happy, well-adjusted adults. Adjustment to the new situation is never easy, but there are things we can do and things we can avoid doing that will help them along the way. This book uses real-life experiences from parents and children who have been through that adjustment, in the hope that they can educate you, the reader, in how best to care for them and others like them.

I have based every chapter in this book around the real story of a child I know whose parents are living separately.

Four of those children are my own and I lived their stories with them. Other friends and acquaintances have been kind enough to share their stories with me. Many names and some other identifying features have been changed to protect their privacy, but the stories are real. (For reasons of anonymity, I have identified many of the children as, for example, girl aged fourteen – G14; boy aged eleven – B11.) In addition I have over twenty years of experience of what children and young people say and think about divorce through my job as an RE and Ethics teacher; I have found the issues that are biggest for them are not always the ones adults think they are going to be. I was lucky enough to be able to do a survey on divorce with over 400 of the children at my school aged between eleven and eighteen. Their thoughtful responses gave me many insights, and I have quoted from them throughout the book. This book is the result of all our experiences, and I hope among its pages you find something to assist you in helping children adjust to their parents' separation. Let's start with Alex's story.

Alex's story
Of all the people I interviewed for this book, Alex was the only one who was quite happy for me to use his real name. I was his tutor for five years, and in all that time he never had any major problems that I was aware of. He was a normal, well-adjusted, happy and helpful member of the tutor group who surprised me, at tutor interviews, by chatting about the fact that his parents lived in different places. He was not at all worried by it. Alex is eighteen now, and more than aware that his friends are finding their parents' divorces difficult, so I was very interested in what had made the situation easy for him.

Timing
Alex remembers when he and his parents all lived together, but they divorced when he was four. So when I knew him, he had

already had a long time to get used to the new arrangements. However, he says he can't remember any real upset at the time. This may be because of his age, although anyone with a four-year-old knows how upset a child of that age can be even when you are leaving them at nursery.

Cooperation

Alex puts the ease of the divorce down to the fact that his mum and dad talked it all through first and planned what they were going to do before they went to the lawyers. The legal necessities therefore came and went as smoothly as possible: there were no court cases and no interviews or difficult decisions that he was involved in or aware of. The actual divorce wasn't an issue for him and has left no bad feelings.

Seeing both parents

When I asked, "Who did you live with?" Alex answered, without any hesitation, "Both." He has no sense from his childhood of losing contact with either of his parents, or either set of grandparents. Undoubtedly, the fact that his parents both lived in the same village made this easier. To begin with the family all lived with Alex's maternal grandparents, and when his dad moved out, he went less than a mile away to live with his own mother. Alex remembers his mum getting him up and having breakfast with him, walking him down the road and dropping him off at his dad's before she went to work. His father then took him to school, which was on the way to his work, picked him up after school and had tea with him. After tea, Dad took him back to his mum's, where he spent the rest of the evening and where he slept. At weekends he spent Friday night and Saturday with his father and Saturday night and Sunday with his mother. Holidays were split between the two. In the long summer holidays every year, he had two weeks with his mum, two weeks with his dad, and the remaining week when both parents were back at work was spent with his grandparents. Indeed, they were lucky to have grandparents on hand for babysitting if either parent went out or away for the weekend.

Amazing, isn't it? When Alex and I looked at the arrangement his family had had, we reckoned he actually did see each parent 50 per cent of the time. (There is a recommendation by the American courts that you need at least 30 per cent access to your child to form a good relationship with them.) Although his "official" home was at his mother's, Alex remembers his childhood as being spent equally with both parents. He has a very good relationship with his father, and happy memories of summers spent camping all round the British Isles with him.

There was a standard arrangement for the big festivals as well. On Christmas Eve, Alex went with his mother to the Christmas Christingle service at the village church, where he sat with his mum, his dad, his grandparents, and all the wider family. On Christmas Day, he woke up at his mum's and had Christmas lunch there, going over to his dad's at about three o'clock and having the evening and Boxing Day with Dad. New Year's Eve was with one parent and New Year's Day with the other, alternating each year.

Finances
Finances were worked out between his parents, with Alex's father paying an agreed amount a week to his mum for Alex's living expenses, out of which she put a percentage (a third) into Alex's bank account for his own use, and which he now spends on clothes and outings, etc. He knows what money he has coming in and what he has to spend, so has grown up with a sense of autonomy in his financial affairs. I sensed there was a minimum of having to play off Mum against Dad to get what he wanted, presumably because the matter had already been agreed and everyone stood by the arrangement. Alex's parents are not particularly well off, and he has always known that he would have to finance any college or university fees. He is looking forward to

studying Marine Biology at a local university on a student loan supplemented with holiday jobs (he's an excellent chef!).

Problems

The only sense of any problem in Alex's life was when his mum decided to remarry. Four years after his parents had divorced, his mother met and married her new husband and they moved away from the village Alex had grown up in. He was about eight at the time and says he remembers "tension". The problem as he remembers it was that he thought the new man was going to try to take his dad's place, and for a while he didn't want to speak to him or relate to him. However, over time, he says, he realized that he wasn't being separated from his father. They didn't move far away and the only difference from their previous arrangement was that Mum now drove him three miles to Dad, who then dropped him off at school instead of walking him down the road. Once he realized that the new man was not trying to take the place of his dad but, as he put it, "was just there", he says he was fine. He now talks quite happily about the good relationship he has with his stepdad.

Security

There was the minimum possible change for Alex in all of this, and a great deal of security. For a long time he remained in the home he had always known and yet saw both his parents every day. He carried on going to the same school with a similar routine to the one he had had before, and he maintained good contact with all his grandparents and both sides of the wider family. In fact, he had a more secure childhood than many of his friends.

As I was talking to Alex, I felt relieved that it was really possible for a child to have so few adverse results from divorce. Alex is, and always has been, a happy and well-adjusted young man. I found myself thinking, "Why wasn't my divorce like that?" This book is an exploration of the things that parents, grandparents, teachers and other concerned adults can do to make things as easy as possible for the children in a divorce.

I asked Alex, "If you could say is only one thing to people whose parents were divorcing, what would that be?" This was his answer: "Remember that even though your parents are divorcing, they are still your mum and dad."

I

Loss
· · · · · · ·

"At least you can still see your dad."

This is what one youngster said to my children when they were talking about our upcoming divorce. His own father had died and his loss was ongoing, irreversible and keenly felt. By comparison my sons were fortunate; they could still talk to their dad, watch motor racing with him, go to the football, and do whatever it is that boys prefer to do with dads rather than mums. To other children, it may not seem that the children of divorced parents have lost a lot. Nor may it be immediately obvious that grief is involved in divorce at all. Yet when I asked the teenagers I surveyed to write down what problems children had when their parents divorced, without specifying what sort of things I might mean, the words "sadness", "confusion", "loneliness", "feeling unloved", "anger", "guilt" and "distraction" came up time and time again. In divorce, emotions are a problem for children. Some of them wrote about practical problems such as "Changing schools" and "Less money", but the overwhelming majority wrote down emotions.

The confusion, depression, loss of self-esteem, anger and guilt that children report on their parents' divorce are all symptoms of grief. Even though I have been through a divorce myself, this surprised me. I always took comfort from the fact that even though I felt I had all the symptoms of bereavement when their father left, at least *my children* still had both their mum and dad, albeit at different times in different places. Sometimes it felt as if it would have been easier for me to have recovered if my husband had died, rather than choosing to reject and leave me. However, my children had not had to suffer those same terrible emotions – they still had their father, didn't they? Unlike their bereaved friends, they could still see him, talk to him and be with him.

I came to realize, however, that while they had not permanently lost their father, they had lost the whole family unit they once had. And in some ways, because of the changes they saw in both of us, they had lost those parents they remembered. I was confused when my children started referring to "Old Daddy" and "New Daddy" because they were talking about the same person. But to them it was bewildering to find "Old Daddy" had been against ketchup with everything, while "New Daddy" allowed it. Old Daddy was happy to be at home with them and Mummy. New Daddy wanted to live apart from Mummy and have girlfriends. Did they refer to "Old Mummy" too – the happy one – and wonder about "New Mummy" who was sad all the time? Much later, one of them told me that they felt they had lost me as well because I was so unhappy.

Now that divorce has lost its stigma and adults take it as a common part of life, we might have lost sight of the profound effect it can have on children. I remember once trying to explain my son's weak performance at school by talking about the stress he was feeling due to my divorce. Yet because it was over a year since I had separated from his father, the divorce had gone off the teacher's radar. She looked confused: "But he still sees his dad, doesn't he?" she said. "I mean, it's not as if someone has died."

In over twenty-five years of teaching in secondary schools I have never known a child to lose a close member of their family to death without an overwhelming sympathy from the staff, meetings to discuss the situation, liaison with the family and strategies being implemented to help the child cope. Schools know that bereaved children may struggle with schoolwork and with random emotions that might surface publicly. Even after some years, there is general understanding if there are some topics the child finds difficult to handle, or if behavioural issues surface. All staff are informed so they can be sensitive to the child's feelings.

However, these excellent pastoral systems have not always swung into action for children of divorcing parents, nor is there always such an ongoing sympathy for them. Yet, depending on the child, the emotional impact can be just as great. Even though no one has died, there are still great losses involved in divorce. There is the loss of the family and the life you all had together. There is usually the loss of everyday contact with at least one of your parents, and there is the permanent loss of that loving relationship between the two most important people in your life.

These losses mean that a child's reaction to their parents' divorce follows very similar patterns to children who are bereaved. It also means that the strategies that help bereaved children cope with their grief can also help children of divorcees. However, children of separated parents have the extra problem of having to deal with the emotions that surround their parents' ambivalence to each other. A bereaved mother can eventually gather her children around her and remember the happy times with Daddy. A divorced mother or father is much more likely to continue in an attitude of enmity towards the child's other parent for some months or years. This makes closure on the loss more difficult for the child. The more conflict there is between the parents, the harder it is for the children to adjust to their new situation.

No bereaved child responds to their loss in quite the same way as another, and no child of divorcees will respond to the divorce in the same way either; but all can benefit from an understanding of the grieving process and can be helped to understand it for themselves. Common emotional reactions to loss are shock, confusion, denial, anger, fear, depression and guilt. It would be nice if the process followed a tidy sequence and we could all say, "That's the shock over; now we'll get on to the anger." At least we would know we were progressing through it. The truth is more complex. While shock is often the first reaction, these emotions could come at any time and in any order, or not at all, depending on the child, the circumstances, their personality and their age. So how can we help them deal with the emotions? Mostly, I think, by bringing them all out into the open. By naming the emotions, understanding them ourselves, acknowledging them as a normal part of the grieving process and allowing children to express them, they become less overwhelming.

SHOCK AND CONFUSION

> *"[Adults should] explain to the best of their ability why it [the divorce] happened, as not only will this prevent most confusion for the child, it will make them feel trusted. Through a time like this, trust is important." G14*

Shock is a normal reaction to an unexpected piece of bad news. It can manifest itself in various ways: shaking, feeling cold, feeling sick, insomnia, loss of appetite, nightmares, headaches and the inability to concentrate. For a child who had no idea there were any problems in their parents' marriage, or who does not understand the concept of divorce, shock will probably be the first reaction. Older children whose friends have divorced parents may at least have considered this as a possibility in their own families if, for example, their parents keep arguing. The more unexpected the news, the greater the shock will be. However, shock can also lead to numbness, almost as though the mind wraps a cloak around the emotions, so for a little while the person suffering from shock may not feel anything very much. Shock always wears off, though, and then the rest of the emotions kick in.

Following on from the shock, or at the same time, the child will be facing lots of different internal questions, depending on their age and experiences. These may well lead to confused thoughts, confused emotions and confused behaviour, so anyone watching might notice the child cries, or is unusually withdrawn, asks questions or goes into a shell, gets upset more easily, or becomes very clingy and helpful – in short, does not behave as they would usually. With so many changes going on and the struggle to come to terms with something they do not want to accept, confusion is inevitable. There is also the issue of lack of closure when parents separate or divorce. When someone dies, there is no hope of this changing. But when parents split up there is the possibility that they may get back together – some do. And while this gives hope it also makes the emotions messier – there is more confusion.

Symptoms of shock and confusion at different ages

Pre-school children

- Tearfulness
- Withdrawing
- Tantrums
- Regression. This is going back a stage in development, which can include:
  - » Toddlers acting like babies
  - » Disturbed sleep patterns
  - » Toilet training problems
  - » Increased clinginess

Even babies can experience feelings of loss. At six months old, I saw that my grandson recognized and loved his mum and his dad and was already forming different patterns of play and behaviour with each of them. If he had suddenly lost one of them, he would have missed them. Very young children don't have the same depth of emotions as older children, but they are sensitive to the emotions of those around them and will respond with tears to sadness or anger in the adults caring for them.

What you can do to help

- Accept the fact that the child might want to be "babied" again.
- Try to keep strong emotions out of the hearing of young children.
- Keep routines the same and as regular as possible.

Primary school children

- Making up fantasy stories and "lying"
- Intense bouts of crying or anger
- Feelings of abandonment
- Bedwetting and sleep problems
- Withdrawing
- Becoming ill
- Loyalty conflicts

Children between the ages of five and seven often seem the most badly hit by shock and confusion. They are at a stage of life when they have a good understanding of what is happening, but are not yet old enough to fully rationalize their feelings. Illness can be the result of a depressed immune system or a wish to be cared for. If a child says one thing to one parent and the opposite to the other, it is because they want to be loyal to both, and is a good indication that they are experiencing divided loyalties. Telling fantasy stories at this stage, especially about their parents' reconciliation, is the child's attempt to work their way out of the confusion.

What you can do to help

- Help the child accept the reality of what is happening, not what you or they would have liked to have happened. Be honest. Be age-appropriate.
- Help them identify and name their emotions so they understand what is happening to them.
- Tolerate the regressions matter-of-factly, e.g. make arrangements to deal with the bedwetting.
- Take notice of a child's real or perceived illness – it's often a cry for help.
- Keep as much of the child's life the same as possible.

Teenagers

- Feeling that their parents are no longer "there" for them
- Attempting to sort out the parents and make it better
- Embarrassment about parents' dating or sexuality
- Feeling in competition with parents
- Chronic fatigue and difficulty concentrating
- Mourning for the loss of their family or childhood resulting in
  - » Withdrawing, refusing to talk about it
  - » Pressure to grow up quickly and leave the family
  - » Pre-occupation and involvement in their own lives and pastimes

Teenagers are on the verge of being adults. Loss at this point can either make them want to withdraw back to childhood or propel them into trying to become adults too quickly.

What you can do to help

- Help teenagers with their confusion by remaining parents to them and not expecting them to grow up too quickly.
- Agree on or maintain usual boundaries and house rules and stick to them.
- Leave the lines of communication open but let them approach you.
- Give explanations clearly and honestly when they ask for them.
- Be age-appropriate with information, especially sexual details.
- Allow teenagers to talk to other people. They often find it is easier to talk through their confusion with their peers or adults who are less immediately involved than family.

DENIAL

> *"Live together, pretend nothing's wrong, don't get divorced." (B14)*

If a child has thought of divorce as something that would never happen to their family, then when it does, it can be so shocking that the first reaction is often to deny it. Typically the adults' disillusionment with their relationship and attempts to reconcile or heal the partnership have been going on for one or two years before they tell the children they have decided to separate. The children then have to take on board for themselves what the parents have already spent a lot of time rationalizing and accepting. The children are right at the beginning of the grieving process. A common initial reaction for them is to deny it is happening, and a normal instinct is to want to stay in that comfortable place of denial. In answer to the question "What advice would you give parents who are divorcing?" one fifteen-year-old boy wrote: "Don't break up – or don't tell them [the children] for ten years. Make something up – they [the other parent] [have] gone on a ten-year holiday to Slovakia."

Denial is a coping mechanism. It protects the child who does not want to believe what is happening. Often the child's first reaction is laughter rather than tears: "You're joking!" Denial can manifest itself as withdrawal, as if the child is thinking, "If I stay asleep or silent, this is not happening." Or it might come out in increased activity, which distracts the child and masks what is going on. Sometimes young children may not want to leave their home at all, even to go to school or visit Grandma, in case the other parent returns while they are gone. Denial can be seen in exceptionally good behaviour: "If I keep my room tidy as Mummy likes, she will come back." Or there may be a doggedness in carrying on as normal: "I'm not going to Daddy's house this weekend. I'm staying here, as I usually do." The last symptom can sometimes be misinterpreted by separated adults, who think that the other parent is trying to prevent or discourage the child from seeing them. The good news is that symptoms of denial usually disappear on their own, as the child gets used to the new situation.

Symptoms of denial at different ages

Pre-school children

- Clinginess and distress when parent leaves their sight for work or just leaves the room
- Continuing to play and refusing to go away from their home with the other parent, or to a childminder
- Checking the cars passing for "Daddy coming home"

- Searching the house to "find Mummy"

What you can do to help

- Keep routines as normal as possible.
- Avoid argument and bad atmosphere at changeover times.
- Allow them to "search" the house for the other parent as part of the process of coming to realize they are not there.
- Gently reinforce the truth, e.g.: "You will see Daddy on Saturday."
- When you are about to leave the child, talk about when you will be back, to reassure them: "I'm going now but I'll pick you up when I've finished shopping, and we'll watch cartoons together."

Primary school children

- Making up stories about the other parent: "Daddy's gone to Disneyland but is coming home soon"
- Making up stories about parents' reconciliation
- Refusing to go to bed until their missing parent comes home
- Lethargy and tiredness
- Hyperactivity and noisiness
- Unwillingness to leave home, e.g. to stay with grandparents or go to school

What you can do to help

- Be patient with any reluctance to accept a change of routine. The reluctance will pass.
- Understand that the stories are ways of trying to cope with an unpleasant truth.
- When you leave the child, talk to them about when you will see them again.

- Keep telling the truth to help them get used to the situation. "You will still see Daddy, but he won't be living here any more."

Teenagers
- Withdrawing into computer games, social networking sites or music
- Oversleeping and difficulty in getting up in the morning
- Staying out late and socializing, spending weekends with their friends
- Using alcohol and drugs to escape the reality
- Refusing to cooperate with access arrangements

What you can do to help
- Keep the normal routines and boundaries.
- Don't overreact – every teenager does these things.
- Continue to protect them from harmful substances.
- Understand that they need space on their own or with friends to rationalize it for themselves.
- Be honest with them about what is happening.

GUILT

> *"Tell them the truth. If it was the child's fault, they deserve to know, even if the parents don't want to hurt their feelings." (G13)*

> *"It makes you feel like you've done something wrong." (B11)*

I was so blind to how much guilt was an issue for the children of divorcees that I didn't even consider it something to be dealt with in this book. I was both surprised and confused when, repeatedly, children were telling me that they felt guilty in the survey responses. "Why would they feel guilty?" I thought. "Guilty for mistakes their *parents* had made?" Irrational or not, children *do* feel responsible for their parents' divorce. I turned to my own GCSE group for help. "What do you think *are* the effects of divorce on children? What sort of feelings might they have?" I asked.

"Guilt," they replied.

"Guilt? But it's the *parents* who've made mistakes – the children have done nothing wrong. It's not *their* fault."

Then one of those generational gaps opened up that neither side could cross. I didn't get it. They didn't get why I didn't get it. After some moments of stunned silence on both sides of the abyss, one brave soul decided to try to build a bridge across it. "It's *their* family," he said. "And they're part of their family… and their family's all broken up. But they belong to it. So they feel responsible… it must be partly their fault."

Translating it into adult terms, I began to see. If you were part of a team working together for years on a project and then that project failed, you would feel guilty. Even if you were a junior member of the team and you knew that the main problem had been rivalry between the team leader and their deputy, you would still feel partly responsible. You might think, "Surely I could have done something differently to make it better." Children feel that way when their parents split up.

Because the parents are seen to fight most over the children or issues surrounding the children, even pre-school children pick this up and feel guilty. They may be reluctant to go to the other parent so as to avoid the "bad behaviour" that makes Mummy and Daddy cross. They may be especially clingy and loving to one parent or the other to placate them over the wrong things they feel they've done, or they may withdraw as if they have been told off, even when the parents are not angry with them at all.

> *"They feel guilty when spending time with Mum
> that they should be with Dad, and then guilty when
> spending time with Dad they should be with Mum."*
> *(G13)*

This makes it almost impossible for children *not* to feel guilty, because whoever they are with, they will be hurting a person that they love. Guilt is therefore especially acute at changeover times or when children hear the other adults in their lives talking disparagingly about one of their parents.

Symptoms of guilt at different ages

Pre-school children

- Feeling Mummy/Daddy is cross with them
- Mimicking the emotional behaviour of the adults around them
- Reluctance to see the "visiting" parent out of loyalty to the other

What you can do to help

- Give lots of love and reassurance that you still love them.
- Keep things friendly at changeover times.
- Don't criticize the child's other parent in their hearing.
- Show that you are happy for them to see both their parents.

Primary school children

- Developing "good" behaviours, such as repeatedly tidying their room, to mitigate the feeling that they are "naughty"
- Becoming anxious at changeover times
- Adopting the attitude of their main carer out of loyalty and voicing it: "Daddy hates us" or "Mummy's mean"

What you can do to help

- Reassure the children that they are still loved and haven't done anything wrong.
- Don't argue at handovers.
- Warn friends and relatives not to speak negatively about the other parent in front of the children.
- Give them permission to see and love both their parents.
- Don't discuss their parents' shortcomings with them.
- Don't ask them to keep a secret from one of their parents.

Teenagers

- Feeling that they have to "become the parent" and sort things out in the family
- Attempting to "grow up" and leave home prematurely, as that is easier than being torn between two parents
- Attempting to mediate between parents, to put right what they feel they have done wrong
- Spending all their free time with friends rather than with either parent. This solves the problem of feeling guilty: they can't be blamed for being with either parent if they do this
- Deciding to stop seeing one parent
- Switching their main residence in order to "be fair" to the other parent
- Worrying about money

What you can do to help

- Remain parents to them and have a joint attitude to house rules.
- Don't use your child as a go-between: deal directly with the other parent.

- Don't use your child as a confidante to talk through problems with your partner.
- Have a clearly agreed system for the child's finances.
- Understand that a child's needs change. Try not to take it personally if they choose to change who they live with.
- Reassure the children that they are still loved and haven't done anything wrong.
- Deal directly with their other parent rather than sending messages through the children.

FEAR

> *"Don't pretend that everything is OK. Make sure the child/ren know what is happening and why, so they don't feel responsible or fear the worst." (G14)*

> *"Parents are meant to be a rock, stable – if they're not, what else isn't?" (G12)*

Children whose parents are separating begin to fear future changes and feel insecure. Knowing they are dependent on their parents, children wonder, "Who is going to look after me now?" and are scared that if they can so easily lose one parent, they might as easily lose the other one, and grandparents and other important adults as well. Groundless fears exacerbate the pain of divorce. When parents separate, children are afraid they too are "divorceable" and can be abandoned. Their trust in adults can be overlaid with a fear that those adults might let them down.

In the absence of clear explanations, children will amplify the pain by building stories around it such as: "I'll never see Dad again", "Mum never wanted me anyway" or "I'll have to leave all my friends at school". Telling them the truth and keeping them informed about what is happening is a great antidote to fear and gives security. All ages of children need to be reassured that although things are changing, both parents will be there for them and involved in their lives in the future.

If you are afraid that you are losing one or both of your parents, it is reassuring to have a grandparent who is there as usual to give you the attention and love that your parents seem too distracted to give. In my survey I asked the specific question, "What can grandparents do to help their grandchildren through their parents' divorce?" Here is a selection of typical responses:

> *"Make sure they have a constant figure in their life, and listen to them." (G15)*

> *"Just don't leave...try and stay important." (G11)*

> *"Try to have [the child/ren] round a lot and provide a stable home situation in one environment." (G15)*

> *"Reassure them that they will be there to support the family – they aren't going to leave." (B14)*

> *"If your family home is not a comfortable place to be, then another home where you feel safe is reassuring to visit, and allows some respite from the insecurity of relationships at home." (B16)*

If the grandparents remain in touch as normal, this provides reassurance and a sense of relief for the children. However, if the grandparents are also upset or angry in front of the child, the child may fear that Granny will abandon them too, just as their parents seem to have done.

Symptoms of fear at different ages

Pre-school children
- Bedwetting and nightmares
- Reluctance to leave the adult they trust
- Regression
- Difficulties in adjustment to nursery or childminder

What you can do to help
- Keep routines in each household as standardized as possible.
- Don't be angry with them for being afraid.
- Remember special toys or security blankets at changeover.
- Have a colour-coded calendar to reassure the child about when they will next see Mummy or Daddy.
- Explain new changes clearly and in advance to the child.
- Warn nursery or childminders that the child may be more sensitive to change.

Primary school children
- Refusing to go to school
- Refusing to go to visit one parent for fear of upsetting the other
- Losing interest in hobbies
- Difficulties staying over with family members

What you can do to help
- Liaise with their school.
- Tell them what is happening between Mummy and Daddy.
- Explain all the new arrangements for their care before they happen.
- Allow ongoing contact with both sets of grandparents.

Teenagers
- Having fears about whether they will be able to sustain viable relationships with the opposite sex in the future: these fears are common at this age
- Reluctance to talk about their parents' separation for fear of being given too much information
- Seeking out premature sexual relationships as a way of providing themselves with reassurance and security
- Suffering from eating disorders: controlling their eating can be seen as a way of controlling their circumstances

What you can do to help
- Reassure them; make time for them so they know they are not abandoned.
- Allow contact with grandparents and other members of the extended family.
- Give the same parenting advice about sex and relationships as you would before.
- Try to keep arguments to a minimum and be as normal as possible.
- Don't discuss sexual details of your relationships with teenagers.
- Find professional help for the serious problems.

ANGER

The experts tell us that it is good to acknowledge all these emotions. Somehow, knowing what you are feeling helps you understand that what is happening is normal in the circumstances. This lessens the feeling's hold on you and enables you to be more in control. However, in our society, we don't always want to accept anger as a valid emotion to express, which makes it the most difficult emotion to deal with in the grieving process. Somehow people expect tears and understand that this is grief coming out, but they don't expect anger or recognize it as a symptom. Children can be angry with themselves, their parents, the world, their friends for not understanding or for still having parents together, and with school for imposing more burdens on them when they already have more than they can cope with.

Symptoms of anger at different ages

Pre-school children

- Tantrums and "terrible twos" behaviour patterns
- Destroying their pictures or toys
- Pushing or hitting other children
- Withdrawing

Primary school children

- Flare-ups of anger or crying over minor issues
- Bullying
- Refusing to see or speak to the parent they blame for the divorce

Teenagers

- Mood swings
- Bullying or threatening others
- Self-harming

What you can do to help

- Allow the grieving child to say how they feel when they want to, and to talk about the situation.

- Don't be offended if they are angry with you or don't want to talk. Handle your own anger as well as possible. If you use angry words and actions, they will too.
- Offer alternative ways of expressing anger – pillows to punch or balls to kick.

DEPRESSION

The words "depression", "sadness", "upset" and "tears" were used in every child's response to the problems of parental separation. For all but a small minority of children, their parents separating will be the saddest thing that has happened in their life. Tears and the other symptoms are a normal response to what is happening to them and their family. For most children, reassurance that they are loved and the support of friends and family will be all they need to see them through their sadness. Grown-ups can find their own means of emotional support but children might not, so encourage them to talk with their friends, grandparents, godparents, adult family friends and favourite aunts and uncles.

As a concerned adult looking on, it can be hard to know when to intervene with more formal help. After all, all two-year-olds have tantrums, and all teenagers have bouts of angst as they grow up and find the world is not as idyllic as they had thought when they were young. Also, every child will grieve differently to the loss of a parent or family: even siblings will react differently.

All children of divorced or separated parents will have depressive episodes. Depression is only a problem if it is very prolonged or when it affects the physical well-being of the child or those around them. Then professional help may be necessary. It's not a sign of failure; it's a sign of good sense and care to offer them whatever assistance is available. Although children do often find it difficult to trust strangers, doctors, peer mentoring, counselling or family therapy may be helpful.

Symptoms of depression at different ages

Pre-school and primary school children
- Lethargy, apathy, no interest in anything
- Feeling "heavy" or "weak"
- Unexplained tearfulness
- Refusing to go to nursery or school
- Lacking interest in hobbies and sports

What you can do to help
- Allow them time to express their sadness.
- Don't expect them to "snap out of it". They can't.
- Whenever possible, make time to listen to them.
- Reassure them that the numbness and sadness they may be feeling is normal.
- Encourage their usual interests and friendships.

Teenagers
In addition to the above, teenagers especially suffer from
- Loss of self-esteem
- Eating disorders
- Sleeping problems

They may also
- Fight with the family
- Turn to violence
- Self-harm

What you can do to help
- Try not to appear visibly alarmed if a child or young person's response seems inappropriate to you.

- Ensure that the young person knows that their feelings are important.
- Help them to feel valued and cared for.
- Explain that depression experienced as a response to a traumatic event such as parents separating is not the same as clinical depression. Encourage teenagers to stay involved with their hobbies, sports and friends.
- Reassure them that you are there for them and that you will listen to them and answer their questions.
- If you become concerned about your child or a young person's welfare, seek the support of your GP.

ADJUSTMENT

If you want to help support a child through divorce be prepared for the long haul. To some extent, like ripples in a pool, the consequences will go on and on for them. However, the good news is that research shows the vast majority (over 75 per cent) of children adjust to their parents' divorce with no discernible or permanent ill effects. They are just as likely to grow up to be the responsible, stable adults you always hoped they'd be. As a divorcee myself, there were times when I feared my children's lives would be permanently wrecked beyond repair. Looking back now (they all turned out fine) I think there are things we can do, and things we can try to avoid doing that will help them adjust. How we as parents and grandparents and teachers handle their emotions can speed or retard that adjustment process. The rest of the book is largely about practical ways of organizing and communicating and loving that will help kids deal with their emotions and speed that adjustment.

LOSS IN SHORT

- Name the emotions – shock, confusion, denial, guilt, fear, anger, depression – so the children understand what is happening to them.

- Accept the emotions the children feel, even anger.

- Reassure them that the divorce is not their fault.

- Try to keep the child's life as normal as possible.

- Grandparents, aunts, uncles, teachers and family friends can help by carrying on as normal, thereby providing a refuge from the emotions in the home.

- The stormy time of emotions will end.

- Encourage the child to find adults and friends they can talk to outside of the immediate family.

- Don't be afraid to find professional help if their symptoms are prolonged or a danger to them.

2

Communication
· ·

"Talk together about why they are getting a divorce!"
(B14)

THE CHILDREN ARE NOT BEING DIVORCED

One of the best ways of minimizing the problems of the emotional trauma of the divorce is to talk about it. From the shock and confusion the children are feeling comes a cry: *"Explain!* Explain to me what the problem is, explain what is happening, explain what is going to happen. It feels like my fault. Explain why it isn't."

After getting divorced, a friend of mine regretted having had his wife's initials tattooed on his arm. When he married again, there was no question of having a second tattoo – just in case. But when he and his new wife had a baby, he had the baby's name tattooed down his inner arm. He realized that whatever happened to his other relationships, he would always be a father. In a very visual way he was communicating to the world that parenthood lasts a lifetime. Parents may divorce each other but they do not divorce their children, and hopefully they will always have a close relationship with them. Yet from a child's point of view, it might not seem like that. "Mummy and Daddy loved each other but now they don't any more. They say they love me, but will they stop loving me too?" This is one of the unspoken questions in a child's mind.

So the survey answers to the question "How can parents make their divorce easier for the children?" were congruous across the ages and genders:

> *"Sit down and talk about it. Reassure them. Don't do it really quickly, but don't drag it out longer than needed." (G13)*

> *"Tell the children what's happening; don't keep it a secret. The children deserve to know." (G14)*

> *"Don't involve children but make them aware." (B15)*

> *"Sit together and plan out what's going to happen." (B14)*

That initial communication of the divorce to the children is going to be a shock even if they have already picked up that something is going on. To some it might be a relief to have everything out in the open. Staying calm is important for their sake, so it is a good idea for the parents to plan in advance what they are going to say. The children may have lots of questions. They may just be shocked. The parents may have been thinking, talking and rowing about their marriage for a long time, but any separation or divorce will probably be a new idea for the children, so they have to start the whole process of sorting it all out in their heads. I have some sympathy with the child who wrote anonymously to me: "What can parents do? Nothing; it's bad enough. Reassuring or anything like that does nothing."

The importance of sitting down and telling the children together recurs in the survey answers. It is not always possible, but the children need both parents to tell them. I can still remember when we sat down around the dinner table with our four and told them what was happening. It was not good seeing the shock and anguish that I had first felt when my husband said he was leaving duplicated on their faces.

Jean's story

Jean was not able to sit her children down because she did not know she was going to leave until she had actually left. Her husband had family in Canada. He was self-employed, getting little work, and their marriage was under strain. She was happy for him to visit his parents in Canada when they became ill, but far less happy when his trips became more frequent and she suspected a new relationship might be involved. When his father died, Jean's husband came back to the UK, bringing a group of friends to stay with him, including a woman he seemed very close to. Jean, still struggling to pay the bills, told him that his behaviour was unreasonable. He retorted he needed his friends to support him and would be travelling to Canada more frequently in the future. Packing a suitcase, Jean fled to her mother's for a few days' rest. Within a week, her husband had filed for divorce on the grounds of her "desertion", taking their youngest daughter along to the solicitor's to state, "Mummy left without a word of explanation."

Tom's story

Tom and his wife, Fenella, had two children. They both missed the partying life they had enjoyed before, and took turns to go out. When Fenella met someone else, she moved out to live with him while Tom stayed in the family home, looking after the children. One night, Fenella came back to the house, drunk, and demanded to see the children. Tom refused, as the children were in bed and asleep, and locked the front door. Fenella smashed the glass, so he let her in. She attacked him, shouting and screaming; then, when he went to settle the children, she phoned the police and said Tom was attacking her. He was arrested – standard procedure at the time. When he divorced Fenella, she was granted both the children and the family home.

Relationships are not as neat as lawyers and social workers would like them to be. In the ideal world, two parents sit down with their children and calmly explain that Mummy and Daddy will not be living together any more and that they both still love the children. In reality, sometimes one partner will continue to love and trust the other, not realizing the other is playing a different game. I know that both Jean and Tom have run and rerun the events of the day when they "left" their children. Neither of them intended to do so; both wonder why they didn't see it coming. Both were shocked at the speed at which their partners took advantage of the situation. Sometimes parents can't sit down together and explain to the children that a divorce is coming, because they don't see it coming themselves.

EXPLAINING IS A PROCESS

This process of explaining to the children and answering their questions is going to continue for some time. If you've missed the initial "telling them in advance" moment, there will be plenty more. Childless couples can have a quick divorce but there is no such thing where children are concerned, as their sense of time is so different. Two years (a normal time to sort out a divorce when children are involved) is a third of a six-year-old's life. Two years is the whole of their GCSE course for a fourteen-year-old, or an A level course for a sixteen-year-old. Five years is a long time for an adult, but for a child it could be half of their life. So handling this stage properly really does maximize their chances of adjusting well, and trying to keep things relatively normal for them during what will seem to them like half a lifetime really helps. The survey I did with the children also brought out that they had found it helpful if there was something positive to be said about the separation:

> *"Try and make [the children] see that they, the parents, are happier now and so it's for the best."* (G15)

> *"Make the child know it's a natural thing that happens in life."* (B14)

The children here seem to be asking for some reassurance that other people have gone through this process before and everyone has survived, and in some cases might even be better off.

ONGOING COMMUNICATION BETWEEN PARENTS

After the initial separation, childless couples need never speak to each other again. But those who have children need to communicate with each other until their youngest child is independent. So it may help to have some guidelines to smooth the way. The best piece of advice I had was to remember that the relationship between the parents has changed. Your relationship with your partner is now more like one you have with a colleague. You are cooperating for the welfare of your children. The relationship can be civil, but it is different from the one you had in the past. It is easy for amicable communication to look like the previous relationship. It isn't. Too much focus on the other parent can raise false hopes or make it difficult to let go of the marriage. This can prolong your confusion and hurt, or the children's. It is also helpful if friends and family can remember this too.

KEEPING THINGS CIVIL

> *"Be civilized around [the children]." (B14)*

If I could say just one thing to divorcing parents, it would be: "Be civil to each other." I know how hard this can be, but try to manage it, at least in front of the children. When I read through the comments in my survey, the importance of being polite to each other when the children are listening came up repeatedly:

> *"[Parents should] try not to argue with each other in front of the child[ren] or complain about their other half to them. It puts the child in a very difficult position." (G14)*

> *"[Parents should] keep their arguments to themselves..." (B13)*

> *"Don't shout/argue in front of [the children] – it might hurt them to see their parents being shouted at [or] maybe physically abused." (G13)*

> *"Stay as calm as possible." (B15)*

The children have spoken. All the mediation services and legal services involved with settling the issues around children after separation or divorce report the same. If you have to argue, complain about or get angry with your ex-partner, don't do it in front of the children. It does them much more harm than good.

Sir Nicholas Wall, who was appointed president of the Family Division of the UK High Court in 2012, has said, "There is nothing worse, for most children, than for their parents to denigrate each other... Parents simply do not realise the damage they do to their children by the battles they wage over them."[1]

As a separated parent, I know the other parent's behaviour often seems unreasonable while my own requests always seem more than reasonable! Nevertheless, any inevitable complaints and anger need to be expressed away from the children's hearing. Sometimes people say, "We've split up but we're still friends." To remain as friends is good, but it may not always be possible. As mediation expert Kathleen O'Connell Corcoran said:

> *Parents do not have to be friends after divorce, being*
> *considerate and business like is more realistic. Treat*
> *the other parent as you would a business partner.*
> *Keep in mind the "mission statement" of this new*
> *business is to raise the best children possible. Consider*
> *how you would behave with a business associate*
> *you were trying to close an important deal with*
> *(you probably wouldn't resort to name calling).*[2]

I find that a much more realistic attitude, and one that is possible to adopt most of the time, or at least when in front of the children.

The Joseph Rowntree Foundation did a review of over 200 research reports in 1998 on outcomes for children of divorced and separated parents,[3] and came to the conclusion that it is not the divorce or separation itself that leads to adverse effects in the children, nor is it the age of the child when the separation occurs. The main factor they found that leads to a poor recovery was witnessing conflict between the parents. That came out in my small survey too. When asked what problems divorce caused, nearly all the children put "Arguments". When asked to list the ways divorce might help the family, they nearly all put "Less arguments".

As we have seen, psychologists say 75 per cent of children show no obvious problems after their parents separate, provided that they have a good quality relationship with both, and parental conflict is not too much or too prolonged. Of course some children of happily married parents grow up to have problems too. Professor Michael Lamb, Professor of Psychology at the University of Cambridge and the world's foremost authority on children's relationships with their fathers, has carried out research on this and says: "Where parents stay together, 15% of their children will grow up with serious problems. When parents separate, that percentage doubles."[4] So the majority of children of divorced parents will grow up with no discernible problems but a significant minority may show long-term problems. The more you can put your own differences and emotions to one side and cooperate with the other parent, the more likely it is that your child will be one of the majority who weather the divorce storm and come through as well-adjusted young adults. Staying civil is often a hard thing to do, but parents all over the world are doing it because they love their children and want the easiest and best outcome for *them*.

MINIMIZING ARGUMENTS

With tensions and emotions in the adults running so high for so long, it is inevitable that those negative feelings will come out in some way. Children may not understand the inevitability of this or the complexities of their parents' relationship, but one of the things they all agree on is that they hate seeing their parents argue. There are various strategies you can employ to help minimize arguments. One or two of them I stumbled on accidentally and were useful: the rest are things I wish I'd known back then.

1. Not in front of the children
Don't bring up difficult issues in front of the children – arrange a meeting when they are not there, or email or phone from another room, or after they have gone to bed.

2. Make an appointment

If there is something you need to sort out, it helps if you are calm first. Making an appointment gives time for your emotions to settle. It may seem daft or even hurtful to have to make an appointment to see your children's other parent, but this is part of acknowledging the changed relationship. It also gives you time to work out what you want to say first. Writing down on a piece of paper the key points you would like to get across stops you being sidetracked. If it's not possible to formally arrange an appointment, then check if it is a convenient time to talk. If not, call back another time.

3. Describe rather than blame

Describing the *problem* rather than the other parent's *behaviour* helps minimize conflict. For example, "We were waiting in the cold for thirty minutes" is better than "You are always late for our handovers". Linked with this is the question of blame: if you blame the other person, they will perceive it as an attack. Attack provokes counter-attack and then you're into an argument. So "What did you do to upset Susan over the weekend?" is likely to provoke a reaction such as: "Nothing! What are you suggesting?" Describe the problem without any blame; for example: "Susan was unhappy when she came back from your house last time." This is much more likely to get a neutral or positive response, such as: "Was she? I wonder why. We dropped her friend Rachel off on the way back to you and they were both very quiet in the car – maybe they've fallen out again." The mystery is solved.

4. Watch out for trigger words

Avoid those words or phrases that will emphasize the hurt or trigger a reaction, such as: "My boys want to ..." "The boys" or "Our boys" is better. Because ex-partners know each other so well, they also know exactly how to push each other's buttons and this can sabotage a businesslike relationship. The word "home" is an interesting one. Your children now have two homes, but this simple word can be very emotive. "When they got back here" or "When they arrived at mine" is less antagonistic than "When they got back home". In the same way, recognize when you are having your buttons pushed – which is usually when you feel defensive. Either turn the conversation back to the topic in hand, or make a tactical withdrawal, saying, "I need to give this a bit more thought and will phone you back tomorrow."

5. Don't interrupt

Try not to interrupt when the other person is speaking: it increases tension and implies that their point is not worthwhile. If you feel there is something you can't let go by, note it down. If interruption is a real problem in your communication with your ex or their family, then maybe you could agree to take turns by agreeing a time limit. For example, "If you'll listen to me for five minutes without interrupting then I'll keep quiet for five minutes while you have your say."

6. Offer a choice

If it is difficult to discuss arrangements for the children, try offering the other person two alternatives to choose from. Make sure before you start that you are happy with either choice made, for instance: "Will you have them on Christmas Day or Boxing Day?" The other parent may have another idea that you both agree on, but the conversation has then begun with respect and without blame and is less likely to provoke argument than beginning it with, "I'm having the children Christmas Day. You can see them Boxing Day."

7. Conclude by agreeing what's been decided

Try to reach a practical solution that you both agree on and can both implement regarding who is going to do what and by when, for example: "So I'll pay for the extra music lessons and you'll get the payment details on Tuesday and email them to me." This makes it clear to both what has been decided and avoids further argument or misunderstanding. Alternatively, follow up the discussion by putting it in writing (email has made this a lot easier and less formal somehow). Write as you would to a business colleague: "Thanks for talking to me about the holidays. I've put what we agreed in my diary that the children will be with me from the 1st to the 10th and with you from the 10th to the 21st." Then you both have a reminder in writing and can refer back to it, should there be a problem.

HOW DO YOU COMMUNICATE WITH SOMEONE WHO WON'T COMMUNICATE WITH YOU?

In all walks of life, you meet people you want to communicate with who do not want to communicate with you. Some don't return your phone calls. Some are drama queens who can only be happy about a decision if they have made a big scene first. Some have to be right all the time. All these reactions and more are seen in and between separated couples. It is possible to learn to deal with these communication problems, to raise matters without blame and to learn to respond to issues without defensiveness and argument. Customer service departments have training in it. Teachers have to learn how to do it with the children in their charge. But it is difficult to use this "business" approach with someone you have been close to. And it is a lot to ask someone to learn quickly, at one of the most vulnerable times of their lives.

One separated woman went to pick up her children from a rehearsal of a play their father had taken them to and he blanked his ex completely. It is not always possible to have good communication if the other parent won't communicate with you. You can only do your part. You are not responsible for their reactions. If they won't answer the phone or talk to you calmly, then try email or a letter. It is one stage removed and allows time for consideration before a reply. But if you are being blocked even in this take advice from Relate, a firm of family lawyers or a mediation service. Professional help in communicating about the divorce – which is an ongoing process that can take a surprisingly long time – is helpful for the rest of the family. It is not always possible to have a calm flow of communication between the parents about the children, but any steps towards this ideal really help the children's adjustment.

ONGOING COMMUNICATION WITH THE CHILDREN

When the divorce is finalized or the separation has actually happened, it is usually an ending of something for the adults involved. But for the children, it's the beginning of a lifetime's process of keeping in touch with two parents who live in different places.

Inform them of changes

> *"Try to give [the children] time to work out why it is happening and to let them get used to the fact." (G15)*

> *"Keep them updated and talk to them." (B13)*

I was surprised from the survey I did at how many children listed "Confusion" or "Not having things explained" as one of the major problems with their parents' divorce. I suppose many of us as adults have lived in other places with different sets of people, changed jobs, changed areas, and we know that it's possible to live happily after a big change. Most children don't know this. Many have lived their whole lives in the same house in the same area, going to the same school, with the same friends around, with the same two parents from the beginning. One boy explained it to me by saying that if the unthinkable can happen and your parents no longer love each other and don't want to be together, what else can happen? Anything! The fear and worry about what might happen is always worse than clear knowledge of what is going to happen, even if that is something you'd rather didn't occur. So it is important to tell the children what is going to happen about moving house, where they are going to live, if other adults will be moving in, and so on. As well as this, children are constantly changing and growing in themselves. What a six-month-old and a ten-year-old can do and what they need are very different. And as they grow and develop, the arrangements for their care and even the home they live in will change too. Clear ongoing communication about what is happening to them is vital for them to adjust to the new arrangements. In fact this is so important, I've given it a chapter of its own: Chapter 9: Changes.

Involve them in decision-making

> *"[Parents] could make sure a child has a say in the choice and be supportive." (G13)*

It is sometimes surprising to find out what the children really want or what creative solution they can come up with when you've tried everything you can think of and nothing's worked. From the really big things, such as which parent they live with, through to remembering where they put their phone, even very young children can come up with good ideas if they are involved in the decision-making process.

One idea is to sit down with the child and write on a piece of paper what the problem is: for example, Jonah and Patrick don't like sharing a room. The writing bit is important: it makes it seem more official. It gives the child the feeling that you consider their ideas important enough to write down.

Then take it in turns to make a list of possible solutions:

Parent: Patrick and Jonah, learn to be nice to each other and never argue again!

Jonah: Make an extension so we can have a bedroom each.

Patrick: Draw a line down the middle of the room and have a Patrick side and a Jonah side.

Jonah: Build a wall down the middle of the room.

Patrick: Send Jonah to live next door!

Parent: Decorate the window end of the room in robot wallpaper for Pat and the door end in Arsenal colours for Jo?

Keep writing all suggestions down, however bizarre or unfeasible. At this stage, don't judge or exclude any of the ideas; write them all down for consideration. When you have got a nice long list, then go through it with the child and cross out all the ones that are just never going to happen (in my example, it would be "Send Jonah to live next door" and "Never argue again"). This helps the child see that none of us can have exactly what we want all the time. Maybe both parent and child would love an extension to the house, but this may not be possible financially. That still leaves suggestions that might just help the situation. Having a role in solving the problem does a lot for the child's self-esteem and helps them understand that their problems have been fairly considered and understood.

Problem-solving with the kids does take time, but is a much better way of dealing with issues than confrontation or laying down the law as in: "Stop arguing with Jonah!"

The Supernanny website (www.supernanny.co.uk) gives more details on the sorts of ways you can solve problems with children, as does that excellent but long-windedly titled book, *How To Talk So Kids Will Listen and Listen So Kids Will Talk.*[5]

PRAISE

I discovered the power of praise by accident at work, surprisingly late in my teaching career. Someone said, "Listen to yourself as you are teaching." I listened and I didn't like what I heard. "Johnny, stop doing that! I am so fed up with trying to hear myself over all this noise." No matter how much I nagged, the class never seemed to remember or improve. In fact, generally the opposite happens. They start to expect that level of nagging from the front and become immune to it, or decide the teacher does not like them – and then they do even less work.

One day I was fed up with marking exams – a boring and largely futile exercise because so many pupils had not bothered to revise. I could hear the lecture I was going to give the class forming in my head: "The vast majority of you didn't learn anything for this exam. It was a waste of my time to mark a set of papers where so many of you couldn't be bothered to learn it properly. Anyone with less than 30 per cent needs to do the whole thing again in detention. I am very disappointed." Then a thought occurred to me: "I wonder what percentage *did* actually learn something?" I didn't want to include them in the rant, so I went through the papers and divided them into two piles – those who'd tried and those who obviously hadn't.

The first surprise was that although there were nine children who really had done nothing, there were twenty-one who had. I had formed the impression that it was the other way round because I'd been so cross with the lazy ones. Then when I looked at their names, they were all children who thought of themselves as being tough or "too cool for school" or they were well known for their laziness. Did I stand a chance of changing their habits of a lifetime? I didn't think so and I was too exhausted to fight, so I decided to forget the rant and just ignore the disaffected ones.

I went into school the next day and did nothing but praise the class – and everything I said was the truth. "I was marking these last night when I suddenly realized that over two-thirds of you had prepared really well for this exam," I enthused. "It was a pleasure to mark most of these papers as I could see you had learnt so much. I was particularly pleased with some of the insights in the second part of the paper. Please come and claim your commendations if I have written a positive comment anywhere on your paper. Don't worry if you haven't done as well as you would have liked; it's only a Mock and there's still time to learn it before the real thing." I then concentrated on giving out commendations for everything I'd mentioned and anything else I could think of. I ignored the ones who hadn't done well and didn't mention corrections or detentions.

So I was calmer, and the ones who had done well were encouraged, which was what I was hoping for. But there was another result I hadn't anticipated. Several pupils came up to me and said things such as: "I did quite well on question one but I hadn't really revised the rest properly. Can I do it again?" or "I thought I knew it but I didn't do as well as I wanted to. Do you still have any of those revision guides left?" or "Sorry, Miss (*Sorry?!*) – I was concentrating on my Maths but I will revise it properly before the real thing." So then in my future tours around the classroom I stopped pointing out the negative things and started only mentioning the positive. To the lazy boy that was behind the rest: "Well done, Darren, you've answered the first two questions already." Staring at the most untidy piece of work I'd seen all day, I'd gulp and say, "You've underlined the title! It makes your work look much neater." To the minimalist worker who's written one sentence to everyone else's page: "That's a really interesting point – no one else has said anything like that."

At first, as I used this approach, I got an oft-repeated question: "Are you taking the mick, Miss?" The answer to this, I found, was to say exactly what it was that was good about what they'd done. "That is very well presented" or "The colour you've used makes your work really stand out" or "That's the best description I've seen in the class today" are all better than "Good work!". The key is to be genuine and specific. Genuine is important. "I really enjoyed that song you sang" is genuine praise; "You're such a good singer you should audition for *Britain's Got Talent*" isn't, unless the whole room was stunned. Nowadays I find some of the laziest or most disaffected children in the school are working well in my lessons and the key every time has been the same: genuine praise. I've found that praise really does motivate children at school and it can motivate your own children at home too.

LISTEN TO WHAT THEY WANT

Good listening is one of the most important skills we can have in our relationships with other people, and one we hardly ever think about. It's also a plea that came out time and time again in my survey. Listening to your children and having them listen to you is so important, I've devoted the whole of Chapter 5 to it.

BRUSHING UP YOUR PARENTING SKILLS

Parenting skills can be difficult in any situation but at difficult times, such as death or parental divorce, children are much more sensitive emotionally. Children can also be selfish and manipulative, and when you are upset it can be difficult to know what is acceptable behaviour and what isn't. At such times, having a few ideas about what you might do about the major parenting issues is really helpful. Most of the time we don't really think about parenting skills; we imagine that it will all come naturally to us, or that we will just do whatever our parents did. Then things suddenly change. I remember thinking, "How *do* you parent at a distance?" I'd had no experience of that in any respect. And how do you handle teenage boys' discipline problems on your own? There are many good websites on parenting that can help with the problems parents encounter with all ages, such as difficult bedtimes, potty training, fussy eaters, talking about puberty, sex and drugs etc. The Supernanny website is excellent in this regard.

COMMUNICATING AT A DISTANCE

It is easier and more convenient for the children if parents live close by, but this is not always possible. The good news is that studies have shown that it is not the amount of time you spend with your children that determines how well they adjust to the separation, but the quality of the relationships they have with you. If there is a large distance between you and you can't see your children regularly, it is still possible to stay in contact. You can even be creative about it. I struggled with this one. For the first five years after our separation I saw my daughters for only one weekend a fortnight. Even though they lived only a few miles away during that time, it seemed like an insuperable distance. Here are some suggestions as to what parents and grandparents can do to maintain contact when time with the children is limited.

Make the most of every celebration
It is vital to remember birthdays and Christmas, to send Easter eggs and congratulations-on-making-the-team cards. Children have a different sense of time to us. Post that arrives the day after their birthday has missed their birthday. Doing some forward planning to make sure things do arrive on time shows you care.

Young children

- Little children may not be able to read but will still appreciate photos or postcards from the places you've been, with a simple message.
- You could tape yourself reading their favourite stories or get the books they like and read to them over Skype.
- Ask to see their artwork and school projects, their bedroom and new pets. If they have their own phone, they can take a photo and send it instantly.
- Arrange to watch the same film or television show, or read a current popular book. Keep up to date with how their sports team are doing so you've got something to talk about.

Teenagers

- Teenagers are in constant contact with their friends on their phones so there is always the opportunity to text, phone or email them and to send photos.
- Talk with your teenager about being friends on their social networking sites and put them onto yours. Sometimes, and on some sites, it's fine. At other times, it's not fine to have your parents messaging you. It does need liaison at this sensitive time, but it is a great way of keeping up to date with what's going on in their lives.
- There is more opportunity for a shared interest with a teenager. I've noticed that boys seem to appreciate doing things with their dads – taking tennis lessons together, going to football matches, joining the same rugby or cricket club. Girls may share a sport or exercise class with their mums too, and also like getting their nails done or going to the hairdresser's together.

Whatever arrangements you make to see or speak to you child, it's really important to keep to them. Children don't understand the complexities of adult life and phoning fifteen minutes late can seem like an eternity to them. It can also lead them to conclude that you don't care.

When you do see your children, give them your time and attention. It is easy to think you have to entertain them or spend a lot of money on them to make up for lost time, but it's you they miss, not your presents. Walking the dog, making dinner or watching a film together can be just as good as a special day out.

COMMUNICATION IN SHORT

- Reassure them that they are not the ones being divorced.

- Develop strategies for communications with a difficult parent.

- Don't argue with the other parent in the child's hearing.

- Don't speak badly of the other parent in front of the children.

- Involve the children in family decisions.

- Don't ask the child to keep secrets.

- Praise them.

3

Organization
· · · · · · · · · · · · · · · · · · · ·

"You have to be a lot more organized." (Abigail, 28)

This was my eldest daughter's first reaction to the question, "How do you think divorce affects the children?" It was not the first thing that came to my mind when I was thinking of possible issues for this book. But as she talked, it became more and more clear, and I was surprised that I hadn't appreciated or seen the effect that the sheer amount of organization needed had had on them as they were growing up.

Let me explain. I'm presuming that you are an adult, in charge of your life, happily settled in your home, your job and your daily routine, as boring or exciting as that may be. Imagine you go home tonight and someone says to you, very kindly, "It's not your fault but from now on you won't be able to live here all week. This is still your home and you won't lose it but it won't be available to you every day. You'll spend Sunday afternoon to Wednesday here and Thursday to Sunday morning in a new home ten miles away on the other side of town. I know you'd like to stay here every day but there's nothing we can do about it. From now on you'll have two homes instead of one. You'll soon get used to it."

As an adult, how would you find that? This situation I'm imagining is not entirely unknown to grown-ups. I once heard an interview with a new female MP about the problems she had encountered. One was how difficult she found it to organize her life in two places. On election night, she suddenly found she needed two homes: to be in London when the House was sitting, and also to have a home in her constituency with the local voters who had put her into office, so they could contact and consult her. Her constituency home was her original home which she had before the election, where her husband, family and friends were. It was also the place where her life was organized the way she wanted and knew. Suddenly she was away from that place for the majority of the week. Although she knew that was what was involved in the job, and had thought about it and chosen this life for herself, she was surprised at the effect it had on her and how much it hindered her life before she learnt to adapt. She was often not sure where she would be when trying to make appointments. While broadly she spent Monday to Thursday in London, and Friday to Sunday in the constituency, sometimes she had to be in London on a Friday, and constituency events needed to be cancelled. Sometimes family celebrations fell on a weekday when she was in London and then either all the people involved would have to come up to London for the evening to celebrate there, or she would have to miss the event, with the inevitable disappointments all round. She employed a constituency secretary to work it all out for her, yet even with this support, she was surprised at how often events in one area of her life impinged on the other, and she felt torn about letting either side down.

If an adult with all their experience in running their own lives and with access to professional help still finds it hard to live in two places and fulfil their responsibilities and relationships in both, how much more difficult and confusing must a child find it? It takes a lot of organization and cooperation between parents to anticipate and overcome the problems a child might encounter daily. Children did not choose the new situation they have found themselves in, and can find it very difficult to respond to it emotionally. They can become more withdrawn, tearful, angry, rebellious or clingy as a result. Parents, however, can definitely help make the divorce easier for the child by taking charge of the practical arrangements. The divorce is much easier on the child if as little as possible changes.

As a teacher and a parent I think of school as a place to learn. Children think of school as a place to meet their friends. Lessons are annoying interludes between seeing friends at break and lunchtime. Most of a child's social life takes place at school. I was surprised to find that teenagers reported one of the biggest practical problems arising from their parents' divorce was losing focus – on both their schoolwork and their social life. The family's problems claim all their attention and there is no room in their brain for other things. So it helps to lessen the lack of focus by keeping them in the same school, with the same groups of friends, if possible. This serves to keep some continuity, and continuity is what they crave as the biggest foundations in their lives are crumbling around them. This comment from the survey was addressed to teachers and sums up this attitude:

> *Try to keep things normal and don't single [children whose parents are separating] out from the class, so that they can relax with friends and not have all of their life changed by the divorce. (G15)*

AN APPEAL TO TEACHERS

This is a personal note to teachers, who are, of course, face to face in the classroom every day with children whose parents are splitting up. As a teacher myself, I know that what we do – or do not do – can make life harder for them, and this is my plea for greater understanding of what these children are going through.

Children are very conscious of anything that makes them different in front of their peers, and that even includes teachers being especially nice to them. Letting them "get away" with things singles them out and makes their peers comment. Some students would even prefer their teachers did *not* know what was going on at home, because they see school as a refuge from the difficulties and they appreciate it mostly as a place to socialize and be "normal".

The response to the question "Can teachers do anything to help?" was an almost universal *No!* This was especially true of the boys, who nearly all put an unqualified straight-to-the-point "No" in answer to this question. One Year 9 boy helped clarify this for me a little by writing, "No, they would make them more sad."

Taken by surprise (I like to think of myself as an understanding teacher), I investigated a little more. I asked my GCSE group about it – they are very helpful in interpreting the language of today's generation for me. Seriously and with some tact they tried to explain it: "Not to be rude, Miss, but you really don't want teachers knowing your business. You probably feel a bit ashamed that your family's failing... and the last thing you want to do at school is go over it all again and have teachers start asking questions..." (General groans at the idea.) I began to get it. It seems that the very clear "No!" was "No! I don't want any more adults going on about it. I don't want the arguments and judgments brought over to school as well. At school at least I can forget about it sometimes." In the words of the one Year 11 boy who did try to clarify it: "Teacher–student relationships can become awkward when talking about personal issues. Don't discuss it if [the children] don't want to, and give them a bit of space."

It seems that the best thing teachers can do is not to mention the divorce, especially in class.

Other comments on teachers talking about the family break-up were:

> *"They just patronize you and are the worst people*
> *to help children. I don't think teachers could help*
> *because they are not your age..." (G13)*

> *"Just letting them know they have someone to talk*
> *to is nice, but to be honest children don't really want*
> *to talk to teachers about family, really." (G14)*

An occasional comment showed teachers could sometimes be helpful in listening to the children: one pupil felt it might be fine "depending on the teacher and if you feel comfortable talking to them". It seems that occasionally a particular teacher will have the sort of relationship with a particular child that enables that child to confide any difficulties they may be having. By and large, however, children want school to be an environment where they know they will not be bothered by the storms of emotions that are going on in them when they think about home. There is one practical aspect, though, that the children say they would really like their teachers to help with. They know that they are going to have some difficulties focusing on class work and doing their homework, and they would like their teachers to understand that, without being too lenient. Their comments reflected this:

> *"Excuse any books or homework left at home*
> *temporarily." (B14)*

> *"Be understanding if work standards take a bit of a*
> *hit." (G14)*

> *"Understand their situation and be easier on*
> *[the child] (understand if it is difficult to finish*
> *homework) as well as ensure they understand*
> *everything in the lesson so they don't fall behind –*
> *maybe give a lesson summary?" (G15)*

> *"Do not pressurize them with work and homework.*
> *Let them be with friends in lessons." (G13)*

Sitting near friends is significant for pupils. Teachers generally are concerned with what happens in that hour they are in front of the children, but pupils carry their hurts with them all day. They realize it helps to be near a friend when there is a lot on your mind. When pupils are very upset about the divorce – which could be right at the beginning or could be three years later, on a significant date, such as their dad's birthday and they can't be with him – they can feel like crying in lessons. It is comforting if a friend is with them at that point. Most teenagers are embarrassed to show their emotions in front of their peers.

Friends are also very good at putting their hand up and asking if a pupil can leave when it all gets too hard. My subject means we often discuss death, divorce, suffering, conflict, bullying and all sorts of things that touch on difficult parts of pupils' lives. Sometimes the content of the lesson is too much for them: maybe because of the overflow of the arguments in the family the night before. Allowing them the support of a friend and some time out to recover is appreciated and helps them carry on with their school life more easily.

Some children also find a time out card useful when they know they might get distressed during the day. This is a recognized piece of card that they can simply show to the teacher on their way out. It gives them permission to leave without having to explain in public what is wrong. If the child uses the card, they go straight to a member of the pastoral team or a trusted teacher allocated to them. Finally, some schools have excellent counselling, listening and mentoring systems.

COMPROMISE AND DECIDE

> *"Let the child/children see both parents so that they still get to have both parents in their life even if the parents don't get along any more." (G11)*

This girl has understood a lot in that one comment. First, she knows that it's the parents' decision on what ultimately happens to their children. She knows that it's a parent's job to look after them. Making the best decisions for other people is hard enough for adults, with all their understanding and years of experience; it's too hard for children to do their parents' job. They want to be involved in the decision-making but they know that adults hold the ultimate responsibility. This eleven-year-old says "let", knowing that it is in the power of either parent to limit the time the child has with their other parent.

In most divorces, at least one of the partners would be quite happy if they never saw the other partner again. Many partners consciously or subconsciously try to act as if their other half doesn't exist. However, it is not the children's choice to divorce either parent, even if the parents want to divorce each other. Most children want to maintain the best possible relationship they can with both parents. Children can and do adjust to their parents splitting up, but that adjustment is made much easier if they know that both parents still want to see them, and if their needs are taken into account. As some pupils said:

"Live close together." (G14)

"Make it so that [the parents] live locally, and the child sees them equally." (B13)

"Always ask for, and respect, [the child's] opinion when deciding with who/where they live. [Parents] don't always know what's best." (G15)

"Involve the children in divorce conversations so that they get a say." (G13)

THE OVERALL ARRANGEMENT

The arrangements made for how much time the child spends with either parent may vary enormously. Usually divorce agreements do not specify arrangements but leave the parents to work them out as best they can, taking into account both the age of the children and the circumstances of the parents. The courts prefer parents to come to their own decisions. Everyone's main concern seems to be to make sure the children are secure and know what is happening.

It is unfair to expect a child under sixteen to decide which parent they want to live with. Except in cases of extreme abuse most children, if given a free choice, want to live with both parents happily together in the same house. But in a divorce, no one is going to give them that choice. Why ask them to choose something they can't have? It is too difficult emotionally. One woman, twenty years after the event, still finds any sort of choice very difficult, having heard repeatedly, "It's completely your choice, darling" at an age when she was not emotionally capable of dealing with that choice. Of course, a child's wishes should be taken into account but the final decision, as with everything else in a child's life, has to be taken by the parents. This is such an important issue for the children and one that is unique to children of separated parents (rather than those who are bereaved or adopted) that I have taken a chapter (Chapter 4: Divided Loyalties) to explain the dilemma in full.

It also helps the child if the adults take the initiative in organizing an arrangement that takes their wishes about seeing both sides of the family into account. As one boy said, "Let the children keep in contact with the parent who is going to live away, and [let them] see the family members regularly." This comment illustrates that children become separated from their grandparents, aunts and uncles, not just their other parent.

When you are at your most grief-stricken and vulnerable, desperate at the thought of losing any time with your children, it is hard to discuss rationally how much time they are going to spend away from you in the company of a person you, at best, dislike. Nevertheless, I am convinced that the more joint decisions you can make with your child's other parent the better it is for the child, because it gives them the security of knowing that both parents care for them. It also allows them to be a child, taking away the burden of decision-making about their welfare. The more you can keep your own emotions and accusations out of the negotiations about the child, the better it is for them. They will not feel then that they and their problems are the cause of their parents' upset.

It is also much easier for the child to accept the new arrangements if the decisions about where they live and when they see their mother or father are communicated rationally and without accusations. They need a workable system of contact between their two parents, and there are various ways of doing this. These are some that have been tried and all have their positive points. Think of the other parent as an asset.

Some possible permutations:

- Share the load as equally as possible throughout the week. This works well if both parents are living locally and have regular work commitments. Alex's story at the beginning of the book is an example of how this can succeed. Both parents need to be flexible and to communicate well with each other.

- A child could spend weekdays with one parent and weekends with the other. This might be a good solution if the children are very young and need the continuity of a primary carer who can be with them every day. The weekends give that person a break.

- They could spend one week with one parent and the next with the other, with Wednesday as the changeover day. When the children are older they can cope with this arrangement well and it means both parents get some weekday and some weekend time with their children.

- How about term time with one parent and holidays with the other? This is often the solution arrived at by parents who live far apart. School holidays may be the only time the children can feasibly travel to see their other parent.

- The children could maintain a main home with one parent and make regular visits to the other. If parents live a long way apart from each other this may be the only way to maintain contact, or be the only arrangement it is possible to negotiate. The advantages of this are that the child has the security and continuity of a real home, while maintaining a relationship with the other parent.

I do not underestimate how difficult it might be to organize a suitable arrangement that all parties are happy with. At one point I was only seeing my girls every other weekend and part of the holidays, and it certainly did not seem enough. It is not always possible for two parents to agree to the ideal arrangement, as what is ideal to one is not to the other.

Statistics have shown that the children recover better if they have a clear and organized routine that everyone sticks to, and if both parents are involved in their lives. The more we can organize this for them, the better it will be.

TRAVELLING BETWEEN HOUSES AND CHANGEOVERS

Peter's story

I love the September term when there are fresh-faced, keen students in Year 7 new to the school. They are generally nervous and often extremely disorganized. Within a few weeks, however, they have usually begun to turn up to the right room at the right time for lessons, and bring their kit to games. It takes some pupils more time than others to get organized but one boy's disorganization persisted throughout his first year without any apparent improvement, despite all the advice, phone calls home and detentions. It got to the point where his chronic disorganization was affecting his schoolwork and progress, so a meeting was arranged between his parents and the school to discuss the issue.

His parents were divorced and had been since he was very young. Both were very involved in his life and keen to solve the problem. His mother's name was down as his primary carer, but it became clear that he was spending one day with Mum and the next with Dad. Each parent had equal shares of his time, so each day was different. And as there are an odd number of days in the week, he could never say, "It's Tuesday today so I'm at Mum's." There was never a regular day when he was at either Mum's or Dad's. Initially, both parents had lived close by in the same village, so it would have been a good, manageable system. Mum picked him up from school one day and Dad the next. As a youngster, he didn't need to think about it. But at twelve the situation had changed quite a bit. Both parents were now with new partners, living with new families, with a good twenty-five miles between them. Now that Peter was at secondary school and more responsible for himself, he had to remember which bus to get on that day. He had either a short bus ride, a ferry across the river, and a walk in one direction, or an hour-long bus ride (with three-quarters of an hour to wait if he missed it) in the opposite direction.

Suddenly I understood why the answer to "Why haven't you got your tie/books/pencil case/homework today?" was "Because I went to my mum's /dad's by mistake yesterday". The problem of "Which home do I go to tonight?" was further complicated by other issues, such as his father working later or his mother going away. This would mean days normally scheduled for one parent would be rescheduled, and everyone got confused. Something as normal as going home after school had now become a major logistical problem for a twelve-year-old. Peter would **genuinely** lose track of where he was supposed to be, which bus he was supposed to catch, or where on earth his school shoes/Science homework/PE shorts/hairbrush or computer memory stick was. This is a story of the difficulties a lack of a realistic system can cause.

After the meeting, things began to improve. Both parents bought a complete school uniform and sports kit so that he could take his uniform off when he got home to either house and leave it there, knowing that he'd have a freshly laundered set waiting for him at his other home. It worked. Dad bought a desk for his room so that he could do his homework as easily as he could at his mum's. Both parents agreed to check he had his schoolbag with everything he needed for the next day before he left in the mornings.

I lost track of him. I hope that his parents managed to change the system for him now that he wasn't a little boy any more. Maybe they went for a week on/week off system, or maybe one of his parents realized that purely for logistical reasons it would be better for him to live primarily with the other parent and they would be content with visits. I don't know. I do know both parents really cared for him. I also know that it can be easy for teenagers to end up drifting from Mum's house to Dad's house to best mate's house and back again feeling that they don't really belong anywhere.

In the words of one of my fifteen-year-old boys, "Make sure they let the child see both parents."

Parents need to take the initiative, and to carry on taking it.

A PLACE OF YOUR OWN IN EACH HOME

When I was looking for a new home, after all the financial details of the divorce had come through, I was concerned about what I would be able to afford. At that point, friends said cheerfully to me, "At least you will only need a two-bedroom home now." They meant one bedroom for me and one for the two children who were with me to share – the other two having their primary residence with their father. Yet my children had been lucky enough to have a bedroom of their own in the previous family home, and I wanted them to have their own space with me in my new house. I thought it was important. In the end I bought a five-bedroom house in a cheaper area so that we could all have our own space. It must have looked extravagant to the friends who were trying to help, but in hindsight I am so glad I did that. It did mean that for quite a lot of the week there were rooms in my house lying empty with the door shut. It also meant that when my daughters came to see me they could open their own door and find their own room where their things had not been disturbed. I involved all of them in the decoration and furnishing of their room and we had all the normal parental discussions about what colour to paint the walls (black did win with son number one), how big the noticeboards would be, whether TVs/computers were to be installed, and exactly how many fluffy toys were "enough" (not son number one this time). At this point, it does help to consult some friends; it's so reassuring to find that wanting to paint the whole place black is a "Goth" or "Emo" thing (pick your generation) and not a psychological result of the family break-up.

If you are not the parent they spend most of their time with, their rooms can look rather bare at first – all their clothes, their childhood toys and their favourite things have gone with them. But give it time. Soon some things find their way back to your house. Football kit comes to lodge with you because your house is closer to the club. Children grow and change and some of their new stuff appears in their room in your house as well as elsewhere. Photos of friends and holidays go up on the walls and the room becomes their own.

It's not enough for most children to be told, "You're always welcome at my house." They have to see that there is a space there for them and they have the things they need. If you put them in the guest room, they will feel like guests and not family. At the time I divorced I presumed my daughters would never live with me again, but I have found that what suits a ten-year-old may not suit a fifteen-year-old. They change. We change. Circumstances change. So when my girls decided (at different times) to come and live with me, their rooms were already there and the transition was that much easier for them. Even now, with all my children grown up and gone, their names are still attached to their rooms in my house. The estate agent might see them as the "study" or "dining room" or "guest room" but *we* all know whose rooms they are. If you do not have enough space to give each child their own room, you can still give them ownership of their bed, their side of the room, their shelf, their cupboard, their pin board, a place in the shed for their bike. Home is where you can put your own things.

Once the arrangements have been decided, each parent needs to make sure that the children have what they need in their home. Research has shown that it is especially important for fathers to create a home that feels welcoming to the children, or an area that is obviously theirs.[1] Maybe we should say "the parent who sees the children the least", which is often the father. Children recover more easily from the shock of divorce and do better if they feel both parents want them and care for them. It is also a real help to the children if parents find some way of having individual one-to-one time with each of them. This is more difficult for the parent that doesn't have day to day contact, but it is worth trying to arrange.

One surprising thing that children say about their family after the divorce is that they get more time with their parents than they did before. I thought logically that each parent would get less time with the children, but the survey gave "More time with parents" as the second most popular answer to the question, "What are the advantages of divorce?" Because two of our children were based with me and two with their father during the week, going into the girls' bedrooms after they had left was difficult. The rooms were bare of all their stuff, and even their bedding was gone. I was stunned into an unbelieving inertia. In the shock, it is so difficult to think of the basic practicalities or to know where to find the money to buy an extra set of everything. But a sensible friend took me in hand. "I know where there is a sale on," she said, and off we went to buy new duvets, pillows and sheets for both beds. We dressed them in old, familiar duvet covers. Having the room all ready for them when they came the next time made it easier for me to bear, and much more welcoming for them. It seems so simple and obvious to me now but at the time it was hard; they already had those things and it was strange to have to go out and buy them all over again.

DIFFERENT ROUTINES

The children's transition between houses will be much easier if, broadly speaking, their routines are similar. The same basic routines at bedtime, mealtimes and getting up in the morning will help; continuity will make the children more settled. If attitudes and expectations about discipline, music practice, training sessions and tidying up are similar, that will help as well. However, it is not always possible to get strong cooperation between parents, even when they are in a stable relationship. If their other parent says the children can eat sugary snacks between meals or stay up late playing computer games and you don't think this is good for them, there is not a lot you can do about it while they are in the other house, but you can at least have your own rules that apply in your home. This may sound contradictory; the ideal is to have very similar routines in each household. If that is not feasible, then maintaining a consistent routine in your own home will help them know what to expect with you.

For example, each parent's attitude to their teenager and sex will vary. Mum may be happy for her sixteen-year-old's boyfriend to stay in her room overnight, but Dad may have a different view. So it is possible to negotiate different expectations in each household on issues you feel strongly about. Children and teenagers are adaptable. They are used to different rules and systems as they go from teacher to teacher in school. Once they get to know the routine and expectations in each household they will adjust to them, even if they are slightly different.

One good idea to help young children adjust is to put up a large colourful calendar where they can see it. Have "Mummy's days" and "Daddy's days" in different coloured stickers or coloured in various shades. Even very young children can understand the colours and help you count off the days until they see their other parent again. It can provide reassurance, as little ones often have some separation anxiety when they leave their home base. For children who find an hour is an eternity, this can really help reassure them they will see Mummy again in a couple of days' time, or it is only three more squares before they go to Dad's.

For older children, it helps keep them informed about what is happening and is a simple visual way to clearly explain the arrangements; "Explain to me", as we have seen, is one of their big cries when their parents separate. It also reassures the children that they are loved and expected. If there is a long time between visits, having the next visit already marked on the calendar is clear evidence that you are already looking forward to when they are coming again. It is a tangible piece of evidence for them that they are wanted. For teenagers, I found a clearly marked calendar and frequent updates essential. At that stage, parents increasingly have to fit around their offspring's many sporting and social activities, weekend jobs and working for exams.

It's even more of a pressure on them if they have two parental households to fit in. A calendar makes commitments clear to everyone, and helps a teenager lose some of the confusion they feel if their family circumstances have recently changed.

SPECIAL OCCASIONS

> *"Make seeing each other on special occasions a priority." (G15)*

Children know that their parents don't get on any more. The one thing they hate above all is their parents arguing. The separation or divorce usually solves that problem, and children report this as one of the positive points of a divorce – the arguments become less frequent, and the atmosphere at home is calmer. In fact, a divorce can make things so much better for the child. Once all the arrangements are sorted out and everyone has moved, life gets back into a pattern again, without the constant arguing. That can only be a good thing. Children miss the parent they are not living with but appreciate the increased attention they get when they are with them. So most children adjust well to their new life and sometimes begin to see real benefits in it – two homes, two sets of birthday presents, and two holidays.

So it's only on special occasions that the difficulties start again. The times that should be the happiest – their birthdays, their siblings' birthdays, Christmas, New Year or whatever holiday you celebrate – suddenly can become difficult unless organized in advance so that everyone knows what is happening. Organizing a way in which all members of the family can share in the special occasion is important. Some families manage to be together amicably at special times. I know families who all share their Christmas dinner and present-giving session together, but most find it easier to organize different days in advance. Christmas Day with Daddy this year and Mummy next, or Christmas morning in one house and the afternoon in the other are both possible solutions.

Christmas with one parent and New Year with another is common too. We had German relations, so it was fun some years to do "German Christmas" with one parent and have presents on Christmas Eve, and "English Christmas" with the other on Christmas morning. I thought my children were amazing, too, in the way they always used to share their presents to each other out between the two houses. It really lessens their anxiety if both parents can agree on this in advance without fuss. Then there are eighteenth or twenty-first birthday parties, school plays, performances and graduations. The child wants both their parents there, but they don't want any rows or "atmospheres". It is hard to ask a divorced or separated couple to be friendly to each other on these occasions, but the more civil parents can be to each other, the easier it is for the children.

Seeing both parents on special occasions is important to children, but having to mediate between them is stressful. Organizing two warring adults is more responsibility than they need or can cope with (just think about the times you've had to mediate between two work colleagues who don't see eye to eye – and you're an adult). Broaching the subject and getting a negative reaction such as "I hope your mother won't be there" or "I phoned your dad but he's being so unreasonable" is difficult too and just makes the children feel guilty, as if they feel they are somehow the cause of the argument or bad relationship between their mum and dad.

Special occasions are not just the obvious celebrations. Fathers especially (or the parent who sees them less regularly) need to be at their children's parents' evenings and to liaise with schools over their children's progress. Letters and reports are commonly only sent to one household, and often that parent is not as willing to communicate or share the information as you would like.

It surprises me that schools are not more aware of this. I

only made it to one of Abigail's parents' evenings because of a chance comment from one of my friends. "See you again later, I expect?" she said, with a rueful smile. "Will I? Why?" I said, thinking I'd forgotten a dinner invite. "Parents' evening!" she said, and then gave me the details that had not been communicated to me. What surprised me even more was that the school seemed confused that I wanted to hear what her teachers had to say as well. "Her father's been in already," they said, but accommodated me as best they could once I'd explained that I hadn't been informed about the evening, but was interested in her progress. It was not a nice feeling.

Things were no better when my younger daughter, Rachel, came to the school I worked in. Although it was easy to liaise with her teachers – they were my colleagues – I was surprised to find that the Year 7 reports were out and I hadn't received a copy. Apparently there was no system for making a copy of the one report issued. "And anyway," said a colleague, "her father's a reasonable man; he'll pass it on to you, won't he?" I got the impression I was being a nuisance and making extra work. After this had happened three times in a row, I went to the head. I hated having to constantly explain to people who had not been divorced why I was upset about something that no one else seemed to think was a problem. I must have managed it, because after that a system was devised to provide duplicate copies of reports for parents who requested them (whether or not their ex was a middle-class professional, reasonable person).

Schools do have a statutory duty not to pass on any information, reports or pictures of certain children who are not allowed contact with one of their parents by the courts, but the vast majority of divorces do not bar one party from access to their child. Often it is presumed that the child will be the go-between with information from school, but this places unnecessary strain on them and puts them in the impossible position of mediating between their parents.

Nowadays good computer systems have helped overcome the problem of information not reaching home. Information about calendar dates, meetings and procedures is often available to all on school websites. Increasingly all reports, merits and de-merits gained, attendance and achievements are kept online as well, with a special log-in or password to access your child's personal information. It really helps if each parent has the means to access this system independently because it takes another level of strain off the child and shows them that both parents are interested in their progress.

ORGANIZING FINANCES: EMMA'S STORY

I was trying to start a sixth form lesson and the girls would not stop talking about whether they were going to a party at the weekend. I tolerated the *sotto voce* discussion for some time but when Emma came out with that old chestnut "I can't go. I've got nothing to wear", my patience gave way. "Oh, for goodness' sake," I said. "That's what all teenagers say – wear a skirt, wear a dress, wear trousers and one of your pretty tops. Just stop talking about it and let's get on with the lesson."

It was some time before I found out she was telling the truth. Emma had lived most of her life with her father, and her mother had little contact with her. He was her sole provider and provided well but, being a man, never really understood the range of clothes a teenage girl needed. Emma had school uniform, shoes and coat and, like her dad, she had jeans, T-shirts and jumpers for leisure wear. But she had nothing pretty in her wardrobe and no party clothes. She nearly didn't go to the sixth form party at the end of Year 12 because she had nothing to wear. So Emma didn't have a wardrobe full of clothes she'd grown tired of, as I'd supposed. She had a divorced mother and father who had never made a formal financial arrangement for her. Mum refused to pay for her keep if she was living with

Dad, and Dad only bought what he considered necessities for her. Emma learnt not to ask Mum or Dad for very much, to avoid arguments, and did a Saturday job to buy the things she needed. However, it barely covered her ordinary expenses. She felt guilty every time she had to ask for something.

In the UK at the moment, all that is asked is that the parents have some agreement as to how the children are to be provided for when their parents divorce. Many solicitors and mediation services have a system on their website that can be used to calculate a fair amount from each parent, and it is best for all if everyone agrees on a workable system. As the children get older and as everyone gets used to being a family in different places, some of these initial arrangements may change and some children will make different choices about what they want. They will be able to make those changes more easily and with less ongoing strain because they will be working from a secure position, if they know it is possible to make arrangements and have both parents stick to them. So having an agreed financial arrangement for the children really helps ease the stress on them initially and in the longer term too. Some parents will never pay anything towards their children, whatever the law of the country states or the agreements made. There are other parents, happy to pay whatever is necessary, who are unable even to contact their children, as the other parent has taken them out of the country. Most of us live with an idiosyncratic arrangement somewhere between these two extremes.

The best agreement that I could get with my husband was vague: he would look after the two children who had primary residence with him and I would look after the two who had primary residence with me. This satisfied all concerned initially, but got more complex as time went on. The children's needs changed, where they spent most of the week changed and both our salaries changed. In the end they were never quite sure which of us they should ask for what. School trips, bicycles, computers, phones, club fees, driving lessons, holidays and college fees became stressful for all of them as they entered into "adult" negotiations with each of us over who was paying. They were lucky in that both of us were willing to pay for them, but even so, they felt the pressure every time they needed something. I never managed to get any sort of system with my ex where we could work directly together.

Friends had a better arrangement for their children. They calculated how much their two boys needed and how much was fair for each of them to contribute, and then they opened an account for the boys which they paid into each month. The boys then knew how much they had to spend. If a particularly large need came up, both Mum and Dad would contribute more that month into the account. As the boys grew up, they were allowed more and more say in how they dealt with "their" money.

ORGANIZATION IN SHORT

- Change systems as little as possible.

- Establish clear systems in your own household.

- The more cooperation between households, the better it is for the child.

- Make a special effort for both parents to be there on special occasions.

- Have a place for the child in both parents' homes.

- Inform schools of the divorce and make sure they inform you of school meetings.

- Parents should decide the financial arrangements and make sure the children are clear about them.

- It's the quality of the time with them not the quantity that counts.

4

Divided Loyalties

· ·

*"Try to make sure the children are not biased against
a parent. Do not make them choose between them."
(G14)*

I expect most people are very naive about the rights parents have
over their children – as I was. One parent is allowed to take their
children and live where they want to in the UK, whether or not
the other parent agrees, provided that the children are well cared
for and happy to go with that parent. Divorce or separation
breaks up a family as well as a marriage if there are children
involved. My ideal would have been to have all the children
living with me, visiting their father. His ideal would have been to
have all the children living with him, seeing their mother if they
wanted to. As in the majority of cases of separation and divorce,
the ideal for each party could not be achieved. The sharing of the
children's time is horrendously difficult for each parent and for
the children. But for the children it sets up an ongoing problem
that their parents no longer have: a sense of divided loyalties. My
survey asked teenagers what advice they would give to parents
who are separating, and much of it addressed this.

"Make sure the children see both parents." (B14)

"Still talk to each other after divorce." (B14)

"Don't drag the children into it. Never stop letting [the] other parent see [the] children unless the child doesn't want to see them." (B15)

"Don't get them to pick sides." (G14)

"Tell them not to leave the children and then contact [us] ten years later via Facebook." (G15)

Most of the young people I surveyed felt that it is important for children to have contact and a relationship with both parents as they are growing up. There are parents who have unlimited access to their children but find the hassle and emotions that accompany divorce can sometimes make it seem as if it would be better for everyone if they didn't see the children at all. This is particularly true if parents are struggling with the depression that comes with loss, or are very conscious of the detrimental effect their divorce is having on the children.

Unless the parent has hurt or abused the child and they need to be separated for the child's protection, the consensus of professional opinion is that all children need both their parents to be involved in their lives as much as possible at all stages. There is a common misconception that if a young child grows up without ever knowing their father they will not miss what they do not know, and therefore will avoid the problem of divided loyalties. Even some fathers believe that this would be in the best interests of their child. Yet child psychologists tell us that it is crucial for children to make strong bonds in the first months of life if they are to develop well emotionally in the future. The attachment bonds formed in childhood have been shown to have a very strong impact on how we relate to others as adults, especially in our closest relationships.

It is in the best interests of the child to allow them to see both parents.

What if one parent is being difficult about allowing the other one access? Careful thought needs to be given as to when it is best to fight for increased rights of access, and when legal proceedings will simply cause more distress and uncertainty to the children and prolong the agony of the whole thing. Each case is individual.

Sir Nicholas Wall is on record as saying: "Generally speaking, children do better in every way if they have two parents in their lives, and the children of separated families are no exception."[1] Sir Nicholas has done a lot to raise awareness of the fact that in our culture the courts and public opinion seem to be weighted in favour of the mother's rights to see their child, often to the detriment of the child's relationship with their father. However, in our ever-shrinking world, it is worth remembering that other countries' laws and other cultures may be weighted differently. In countries and communities strongly influenced by Islam or Orthodox Judaism, it is the father's duty to make sure his children are well cared for, well brought up and well provided for. To be a good father in these cultures, a man would be expected to have day-to-day care of his children, to the detriment of the mother's rights. If we try to exclude either mother or father from a relationship with their children, we run the risk of damaging the child's emotional development and, far from solving the sense of divided loyalties, this approach can often just postpone the problem until, in young adulthood, it can become much bigger.

Over the years I have got to know numerous teenagers who are missing their dads often because it was decided very early on that it would be better for all if they were not involved in their lives. They want to know their fathers, even if their mums don't want any contact with them. The emotional strength required to leave the parent who has brought you up in order to go to live with the parent you have never known causes the most extreme pain regarding the divided loyalties that the teenagers talk about. What I have noticed is that children are much happier if they can at least visit their other parent (often fathers) even as little as once a year (some fathers live abroad). It is still important to them. Even the teenager who met his father only six months before the dad died was so pleased to have done it, and his only regret was that it hadn't been sooner.

Cultural and legal differences mean that every year thousands of parents abduct their own children and return to their home countries where the law may be more sympathetic to their point of view. In the most extreme cases, parents take their children away to another country without informing the other parent. This is illegal and needs the help of a specialized lawyer. Reunite International (www.reunite.org) offers support in such cases, and the Ministry of Justice at www.justice.gov.uk has an International Child Abduction and Contact Unit. I think any court anywhere in the world would have to have the wisdom of Solomon x 1,000 to work out what is really just and unjust in each individual situation, but it is important that the children involved have the option of contact with both parents.

INCLUDE THE CHILDREN

> *"Give [the child a] choice of who [they] would rather stay with." (B15)*

I was surprised by the number of children in my survey whose comments implied that they had not really had any say in which parent they lived with. Including the children in the decision-making and trying to arrive at a decision with them is difficult in such a fraught situation, but it helps the child overcome those terrible feelings of everything being out of control if they feel they have a say in what happens to them. On the other hand, I also had comments such as: "Be civil, explain what's going on and don't make them choose." How can you let them choose and yet not make them choose? I think the way you communicate with them and discuss the whole situation is very important. They want to have a choice but they don't necessarily want to have to choose one parent over another, especially if they feel that will be held against them in some way. In the end it comes down to the age and sensitivity of the child, and the individual situation. Overall, the more inclusion you can achieve without overburdening the child, the easier it will be for them to adjust to the new situation. I think the cry of "Don't make them choose" is symptomatic of the hurt that comes to children from parents playing "push-me-pull-you", as we are about to see.

PUSH-ME-PULL-YOU

"Don't accuse [a] child of 'taking sides'." (G13)

One thing that children hate and find very difficult to deal with is what one of my boys used to call "playing push-me-pull-you". For example, it is a bank holiday, not one of the holidays usually divided up. When the children say they are going over to Dad's for the day, Mum says, "I've defrosted that big joint and I can't eat it all on my own." Or the children come home excited because Mum has told them they are going to Disneyland Paris. Dad says, "Wait until the holidays and I'll take you to the proper Disney World in Florida."

Children find this difficult to cope with, but struggle to explain why. Psychologists call it being in a loyalty bind. In the survey, pupils said, "Don't use children as leverage," and, "Don't use them to hurt the person you're divorcing." Parents argue over their child because they both want and love them. But because the parents are arguing and upset, and because the child is the cause of that, the child feels guilty. Children describe this as feeling "torn", and it is a violent feeling. Thinking about it, there is no way the child can win in this situation. Whatever they do, one of their parents is going to be upset with them for not spending more time with them or choosing them. They are being put in an impossible position. Instead, it is much better to do what this youngster recommends: "Keep them informed about what is going on, and try to make sure the children are not biased against a parent."

Any sentence that starts with "Tell Daddy I…" is a push-me-pull-you sentence. You are making the child your representative, expecting them to put your point of view to their father, who may not like or agree with that message. They also then become the recipient of the other parent's reaction, making things very difficult emotionally for them. Pupils said, "Keep the children out of it. Don't use them as messengers and don't argue in front of them." Don't send messages to the other parent via the children either verbally or by letter. This seems odd at first, especially after a lifetime of saying "Can you tell Dad to get some milk on the way home" or "Remind Mum it's football practice on Wednesday". But when the relationship between you is not close and loving any more, relaying messages puts the children right in the firing line. What if they forget the message or lose it or say it in the wrong tone? And if the reaction to the message is bad – "What do you mean, Dad can't look after you on Saturday?" – it is the child who suffers and feels at fault.

DON'T ASK THEM TO KEEP SECRETS

Asking a child to keep a secret from their other parent is asking them to take sides. Although your ex is no longer part of *your* family, they are part of the *children's* family. We can as parents ask our children to keep things secret from strangers. "Don't tell your friends we're moving just yet" is fair enough – it's not their business – but "Don't tell your mum we're moving just yet" is in a completely different category. Children usually feel a strong sense of loyalty to both their parents, so being expected to keep secrets from them places the children in a very stressful position. If there is something you want to keep secret from the other parent – for instance, the state of your finances, where you are going on holiday, what colour you're painting the lounge – then don't share that secret with the children either.

Other push-me-pull-you sentences could be "Your father never keeps his promises" or "Your mother's always late". Children love both their parents and it hurts them as much to hear you put their mother or father down as it would if they heard someone put *you* down. This goes for grandparents, aunts and uncles and friends too. They may all have very strong views on the rights and wrongs of the behaviour of one or both of the parents, but sharing those views with the children hurts them. It can also sow seeds of doubt and worry in a child's mind. Children know that they are biologically made from their parents. They share half their DNA with each parent. They have similar characteristics. Whatever you accuse one parent of you are actually accusing the child of as well. "Your mother's a liar" is saying to the child "You are the son of a liar", which is tantamount to saying "You are a liar like your mother". "Your father always did have anger problems, and look at all the harm it's caused" may sound as if you are just stating the truth about your ex, but it could lead to your child worrying that they are going to turn out angry like their father.

When two adults separate, it is tempting to tell the children all the details of your partner's subtle and not so subtle deficiencies. But they will work out what is true for themselves as they get older. Trust your children. Denigrating a child's parent is saying to them "You are wrong to love your father/mother" and they are not. It is also saying to them "I hate half your DNA. Half of your characteristics are wrong" and they are not. A child is not responsible for the deficiencies of either of their parents, but they will *feel* responsible if they continually hear other adults they love talking about those deficiencies, whether they be their parents, grandparents, family friends or aunts and uncles. There is a place for the truth. The child who wrote, "My parents don't live together because Daddy gets angry when he's had too much to drink," obviously had had a sensible adult talking to them and helping them put the truth into suitable words, but usually talking negatively about their other parent just delays the child's adjustment. If you denigrate your ex-partner you are teaching the child that that is OK and they will start to do it too. But it will work both ways and they will start to think it is OK to denigrate you as well. You can't stop the stories and lies that the other parent may tell about you, but you can at least demonstrate yourself that this is not acceptable adult behaviour. Or as one sixteen-year-old girl expressed it: "Stay on good terms: no bad-mouthing the other parent to the child. Be mature and sort out problems like adults."

This isn't the same as denying the truth. As children mature they will come to understand each of their parents for themselves. If they say to you, "I don't like Mummy getting drunk. I've told her but she takes no notice," then there is a place for acknowledging the problem and the effects it has had on you both, but this can be done without denigrating the other.

Because children love both their parents, they very often need "permission" from one partner to have a good relationship with the other. They don't want to hurt either of you. They don't want to be the cause of any more hurt in the family. After all, if you said, "I really don't like your friends. I don't like their behaviour. I don't like what they get up to and I think they are a bad influence on you," any loving child would stop meeting those friends, or feel very guilty if they did so. Hurt people all over the world say many worse things about their previous spouses.

TRANSITIONS

Children can be especially sensitive at transition times, when one parent hands them over to the other. They may get upset and refuse to go. This may be because they don't really want to see their other parent because they are tired, can't be bothered to get ready or are involved in what they are doing and don't want to be disturbed. It may be they know you will miss them and they don't want to let you down. It might even be that they like to be the centre of attention and playing up about the visit gives them control. Transition times are also one of the few times when parents see each other and the tension at this time will be felt by the children.

When an argument starts at transition time the children will deduce that it is their fault. Most children report that one of the best things about the divorce is fewer arguments in the house and their parents are generally happier. If the only time they hear their parents arguing or feel tension in the air is during handover times or when the parents are trying to discuss something to do with them, the child will feel responsible for the aggro (it was, after all, about them). They will again feel torn in two (whichever side they agree with, they are going to hurt someone) and guilty (if they weren't there, their parents wouldn't be so upset).

I didn't really realize how much this affected my own children until much later when they were able to explain to me what it had been like. Even though we had no big rows in front of them that I remember, they were very aware of tension between us. Children do not understand the complexities of adult relationships, but they do get upset by those feelings. So the more you can keep communication calm and civil between you and your ex-partner, the better the children adjust to the new situation.

Transition times are hard. I found it difficult to return my girls to their father after their weekend visits to me. I used to drop them off and watch them go inside from the car, and would try to smile as they waved goodbye at the door. I am sure they sensed I was unhappy. The unhappiness or anger or irritation that children feel between their parents at transition times can provoke a real sense of divided loyalties in them. Dropping the children off at the front gate can be a real help, as it avoids that direct contact with the ex-partner.

As they got older and had a phone with them, the children increasingly took control of the transition times. They would get a message on their phone that Daddy was waiting outside and could then say goodbye to a happy mummy in the house and go to meet a smiling dad in the car. If face-to-face contact is difficult at any stage of the proceedings, then some simple strategies to avoid it can also avoid the atmosphere and potential arguments there could be at transition times. When you do meet in front of the child, this fourteen-year-old boy's advice is: "Don't argue... Smile. Act like friends." For some parents "acting" will be all they can do, but it is worth it for the children. Other parents eventually do manage a friendship post-separation.

This fifteen-year-old girl realizes the benefits as she says: "My advice is [that] the parents try not to hate each other, because my mum and dad are like best mates or brother and sister, so it's better."

PARENTING AT A DISTANCE

One of the hard things to come to terms with is that your child will have a life with their other parent that you are not a part of. It is tempting to ask a lot of questions about what they did and didn't do while they were away, but this puts the child in a difficult position. They may feel that it is not OK for them to have enjoyed themselves. Because they love and respect both parents, they are loyal to both and feel strongly that it is disloyal to talk about what happened in the other parent's house. As a divorced parent, your control of what happens to the children does not extend into your ex-partner's house and neither does theirs into yours.

It's a strange feeling. It is a bit like when the children first went to school. Just as I couldn't tell their teacher how to organize their school day, I could not tell my ex-husband how to organize his home, and vice versa. From time to time you will hear complaints from the child about the other household. It'll be a real problem, but it will be coming through the child's lens of hurt and will often be exaggerated – or at least it will be by the time it gets to you. It will also be coloured by their insecurities and their wanting to gain favour with you. Children in the best home situations become adept at playing one parent off against another, unless the parents present a united front. Moving between households gives plenty of opportunity for children to hone this manipulative skill into a fine art. A way round this is to make it clear that what goes on in the other household is the responsibility of the other parent, and that you are confident your child can work it out with them. Say something such as: "Well, maybe Mummy doesn't realize that you think seven o'clock is too early for bedtime. Why don't you talk to her about it and see what the two of you can work out?"

I see evidence of a child's manipulative skills a lot as a teacher. For example, "Waynetta, why are you eating in the classroom?" "Mr Smith said I could." I hesitate (mistake) and in chimes her best friend, Henribella: "He did, Miss! He said he didn't mind because it was our form room." The smiles are genuine, the girls are lovely, and the manipulation works nine times out of ten. The tenth time I actually ask Mr Smith, who, of course, has never given such permission. The manipulation works because Henribella and Waynetta are relying on the fact that I will be too busy or too reluctant to actually speak directly to the other adult involved. So if you are seriously worried about what your child has reported to you from their other household, then contact the other parent directly, preferably at a time when the children aren't around, and when you are feeling calm about it.

It didn't always work for me, but at times it did. During the period our children were being brought up in two households, their dad and I discovered in this way that *neither* of us had said, "Well, if your mum/dad won't let you have the tattoo, I will," that we had *both* paid for the school trip that the other one was "too mean" to pay for, and that neither of us had signed the "permission to leave school to go to the dentist" form. We also discovered more than once that when our teenager had said "I'll be at Dad's" to me and "I'll be at Mum's" to him, she was actually elsewhere. Children will push the limits as far as they can; sometimes to see if you really love them, sometimes to see just where the limits are, and sometimes because they just can't see the dangers adults can see. The more you can communicate and cooperate with the child's other parent, the more secure and safe the child will be.

The fact that there is another household that the children can go to can be a real asset. Although at first it was really lonely and strange to be in an empty house when everyone was away, it did give me that opportunity for time to myself, time that I really hadn't had through four children and sixteen years of motherhood. I used the times the children weren't there to see my friends, to catch up with the inevitable backlog of marking and schoolwork, to tidy up the house or garden unhindered, or to go away for a break. As teenagers, they tended to bring their worries about schoolwork and exams to me but their worries about driving lessons and cars to their father, which was a relief!

Some parents feel the responsibilities of childrearing are not adequately shared, and wish their ex-partner would take more of a role. Don't be afraid to use their father or mother as a resource when you need an evening off or a break. However, never allocate your ex-partner's time or resources without their permission. Your relationship with them does not extend that far any more.

Instead, for example, if your child gets an invite to a friend's sleepover on a day when they are not with you, get their friend's parents to make the arrangement with your child's other parent.

Strangely (to me at least), children report that one of the benefits of divorce is an increased resilience and strength in themselves and an empathy for other people. Resilience, strength, independence and increased sympathy for others are good qualities in our children. Learning at first-hand that people organize their lives differently can be an advantage to them in their future lives. Divorce can also bring the parent and child closer together, even if the parents themselves are further apart, as the children get more quality time with each parent on their own.

GRANDPARENTS, AUNTIES AND UNCLES

Although I've written generally in this chapter about the parents from the children's point of view, everything I've said also applies to grandparents and other family members. When I asked the children "What can grandparents do to help?" I was expecting answers such as "Invite us round to tea" and "Take us away on holiday", and those were some of the responses I received. But I also had a lot like this too:

"Don't talk bad about either parent." (G15)

"Tell [grandparents] not to try and turn them against either of their parents; just be sympathetic." (G15)

"Still be there and still acknowledge the child as their grandchild." (B15)

"Check [the children are] OK, but don't take sides." (B14)

"Offer to care for them when parents are arguing.
Encourage them; tell them it's going to be all right."
(B13)

"Give them biscuits!" (B13)

When one of your own children is involved in a divorce, it
can mean that it is more difficult or awkward for you to see
your grandchildren. Your own children will want your support,
but the grandchildren will want you to be neutral. From
the grandchildren's point of view, they want their lives to be
peaceful, stress-free and unchanging. If grandparents (and
wider members of the extended family) can offer a sympathetic
haven (with biscuits) without showing a strong preference for
one parent or the other, the children with love them for it and
will have a respite from the divided loyalties they feel. If you
simply offer them more of the same tensions and arguments
they are getting at home, you won't see them very often, and it
won't be their "other parent" who's keeping them away.

When you can't see your child or grandchild regularly there
are ways of staying in contact, all of which we shall cover in the
next chapter.

DIVIDED LOYALTIES IN SHORT

It helps children if:

- both parents are involved in their lives;

- there is a businesslike relationship between the two parents;

- they are not used as messengers;

- the changeover times are civil and argument free;

- you don't use them as leverage to get what you want from their other parent;

- grandparents, extended family members and family friends don't take sides.

5

Listening
· · · · · · · · · · · · · ·

"It's still affecting me today ... it's left me with issues
about trust, and I'm more cynical."

So said my youngest daughter, now twenty-four, when I recently
asked her about the family break-up. Maybe it's this adult way
of thinking that makes us ask things such as "Have you got used
to it now?" after six months, or "Are you happy now?" after two
years. It is surprising how soon adults generally forget what has
happened to the child, and forget that they are still living with
the consequences.

Gemma's story

Gemma asked to talk to me one day at the school where I worked,
because she was worried about having missed a deadline. When
I asked her why she'd missed the deadline, she told me about
the awful time she'd been having at home. Her parents had
been separated for two years, the divorce was finally through
and Gemma had helped her dad move into his new house that
weekend. However, as she was helping, it became clear that a
certain young lady was going to be living in the new house
with Daddy. This was the same young lady that Daddy had
been telling her (and her mum, her sister and the divorce court)
for the past two years was "just a good friend", and Gemma

had believed him. To cap it all, Gemma's sister announced that weekend that she was going to live in the new house with her father and his girlfriend. Gemma could only think of the day she'd told her Dad that she would never speak to him again if the rumours about this lady turned out to be true. Gemma was a very bright and conscientious student but she had not given her homework any thought over that weekend, or for quite some time. Instead, her head was churning with what was happening to her family.

On the very same day, I went to the staffroom to eat my lunch and was met by a colleague. "I need to speak to you about Gemma," she said. "We need to take a firm hand with her. Her results in the Mock were dreadful … she's an A* student but she only got a B and she's not done any work for weeks."

"She's having a difficult time at the moment," I tried to explain.

"Yes, I know her parents split up, but that's all over now; she can't keep using 'family problems' as an excuse for not doing her work. That was years ago."

She was correct in that Gemma's parents had split up two years previously. She was incorrect in thinking that because two years had passed everyone would be settled either practically or emotionally. Huge issues were still upsetting everyone. I used to think that two years marked a time when it was all over. Now I think in some ways that after two years you're hardly over the beginning.

Think about it from Gemma's point of view: it was over two years since her parents separated, but that particular weekend marked the day that the family split became visibly permanent. Instead of being in temporary accommodation, her father was in a new house and a new relationship. Her sister was now leaving as well, and Gemma had to cope with a mother who was even more upset than usual because she had just found out that her suspicions about the other woman were true. Gemma also had her own issues about how far she could trust what her father said. She did get her work sorted out, and she did get very good GCSEs and A levels. But at that particular point, she was struggling, All she needed was someone to listen to her and acknowledge what she was going through, and perhaps one or two practical suggestions about how to catch up with her work.

LISTENING

"I think you've just got to get it all off your chest."

That's what Rachel said to me when I asked her how she dealt with those issues of trust and cynicism about men that she had identified in herself. And to do that, you need someone who is prepared to listen. The first difficulty in real listening is the emotional one. If you are listening to the symptoms of grief that we outlined earlier, then you will be listening to sorrow, anger, resentment and irrational fear. There might be tears; not over something that happened today, but something from years ago. There might be anger; not the anger of the twenty-year-old in front of you, but the anger of the five-year-old who felt it but had no means of expressing it at the time. In short, you will be in the presence of a lot of emotional pain. The person "getting it off their chest" (and it does sometimes feel like a solid weight stuck inside you) cannot do that unless there is someone to listen. On the other hand, the person may talk to you quite dispassionately, sometimes expressing some unbelievably hurtful things in a matter-of-fact way. It's all part of the grieving process.

The Buddhist teacher Joan Halifax in her compassionate book, *Being with Dying*, says:

> *In these kinds of situations, we want so much to do something. We can feel helpless, heartbroken, angry, and confused. What really can we offer, we ask? The*

treasure many of us forget is our presence. Often there is nothing to do but be present for pain just as it is.[1]

She was writing about supporting someone through bereavement, but the same skills of listening are needed in supporting someone who is grieving because they have lost someone through divorce. Being present is an important part of listening. Just being there helps. Listening is difficult to do. Most people who are really listening think that they are doing nothing. "I only listened," they say when thanked for their help. But it is exactly that which is so helpful. It's not so much what you *do* but what you *don't do* that's so important.

Listening is not the same as giving advice.
Most of the time when your children talk to you, they are not asking for advice. If they do want advice, they will ask directly for it: "What's the best phone to buy, Dad?" "Should I have a year off before going to uni, Mum?" Giving advice is one of the useful roles parents and grandparents have, but it is not the same as listening. Sometimes all children want is someone to understand and acknowledge what they are going through. I've found that if you keep offering advice ("You could do this... you could say that...") they'll ignore it and just keep repeating themselves with increasing frustration. They don't want the advice. They've already been through all the scenarios you can think of and rejected them in their heads loads of times. They want you to show you understand what they are saying or feeling.

Listening is not the same as having a conversation.
If you are really listening to someone, you limit your own talking. When the other person is speaking, if you are really listening you are not thinking in your head about what you are going to say next. It's also not jumping in with connections that

you think are relevant. "I saw a programme about that" and "My friend Theo said that too" are good comments if you are having a conversation, but they are interruptions if you are listening. It takes patience while the child is struggling to put alien feelings and ideas into words. Listening means not jumping in to agree or disagree, or to say for them what they are trying to say.

Good listening means keeping a check on your own emotions. I think that is why children often go to people who understand their situation but are not directly emotionally involved, such as their own friends who've had parents who've divorced, or a sympathetic family friend or grandparent. But even friends and relatives can have strong emotions. If a child tells you something about a parent and you follow it with "Yes, I know. He's always been a devious and manipulative liar ever since I've known him" or "How could she do that to your poor father? She was a terrible wife", it really isn't going to help. It just adds fuel to the fire and increases the child's confusion. The more parents, friends and relatives can keep the strength of their own anger, hurt and resentment out of their conversations, the easier it is for the children to talk and the easier it is for them to get over whatever is bothering them. By talking they are trying to dispel the strange atmosphere and tension. If talking only creates more anger and tension in the adults they are talking to, they'll stop speaking. I know, believe me, that it can take a great deal of self-control to speak about one's divorced partner or daughter-in-law dispassionately, but the more one can maintain a gracious attitude, the more the child will be free to talk. For a parent, the divorce means a cutting of ties to the other person, but the child can never cut their genetic inheritance. The more you put their father or mother down, the more you are putting them down. This links with the next point.

Good listening is non-judgmental.
No child will tell you anything that worries them about their mum, dad, family or the situation if they think you are going to be judgmental. We may need to listen to the child's view of their mother or father's behaviour or character without imposing our own. We can tell we are being judgmental when we use words such as "should", "ought", "must" and "don't"; for example, "Daddy should have arrived on time", "Don't say that about your mother; she's trying her best", "You ought to try to see it from her point of view" or "You must try not to get so upset". Giving a judgment on what has been said (even if it's a good one) is the opposite of acceptance, and no child will talk to you if they don't feel their views will be accepted.

Good listening is acknowledging what has been said.
A good way of doing this is by trying to summarize what has been said so far, and offering it back as a question. Something like: "So, do you mean you wish Daddy had been on time?" Putting it as a question is not the same as a judgment; you are not telling them what you think, you are asking them if that's what they meant. This helps the child, whether you've got it right or wrong. If you've got it right, they will look relieved, and say something like, "Yes, that's right. I do wish he had been on time. He keeps being late." You've helped because they've been heard and you can identify why they felt so strange. If you've got it wrong, they'll respond with, "No! I don't mind if Daddy's late. I just want to see him more often." Again you've shown them that you have been listening, and you've also helped clarify something for them. Very often, though, nothing more is needed than a simple "Mmm" or "Yes" or "I see". It sounds like nothing but it lets them know you are really listening to them.

Good listening is recognizing the opportunity.
We sometimes expect our children to be emotional, especially in the early days, but instead they are passive and withdrawn and don't want to talk. Sometimes children are reeling from an emotional overload, and they don't want to keep talking about it. Or if they do, they don't want to get all worked up about it again; it's just too exhausting to live with that turmoil of feelings. However, sooner or later they will want to talk about it.

You can't make anyone speak to you. With children it often comes out when you are doing something completely different. I remember making the washing-up stretch for as long as I could, reaching for everything in sight and deciding to clean the vases and scour the chip pan as well because my son was talking to me. Once I was deadheading the flowers rather aimlessly in a border when my daughter came and started speaking to me. By the time she had finished, there was hardly a flower to be seen on the bushes, and every single tiny weed had gone as well.

When they are ready to talk, they need someone who will just listen. Doing some ordinary activity at the same time seems to take the intensity out of the situation and helps them talk. You can't engineer it, but you can recognize it when the opportunity arises. Feeling that you have to rush on to the next thing is not conducive to good listening. Maybe that is why grandparents can be so good at it; they are one stage removed from the intensity of everything and they usually have more time.

Good listening is done with a caring heart.
Children know whether you really care about them and their issues or not. I think that is why so many children don't choose to accept any formal counselling, even when it is offered. They are afraid of an official or authoritarian attitude. For the same reason, because they are in authority, teachers aren't the best people to listen to a child unless they have a really strong relationship with them. I am informed by some of my children

at school that "even cool teachers" come across as awkward when trying to assist in a personal way. It's the relationship the child has with the adult that counts, more than the position they hold.

Children may need someone outside the family to listen.
Children naturally start having important relationships with other people besides their parents and family between the ages of about nine and thirteen. When the parents divorce, it will often be good for a child to talk to someone outside the family about their problems and feelings. It can really help to let the child know that's OK with you, or who it's OK to talk to. Sometimes family members, for obvious reasons, are very sensitive about children talking to people outside the family, but if there is at least one person the child can trust or talk to, it can be very helpful to them. I am very grateful for the godparents, relatives and family friends who listened to my children when there were things they felt they could not discuss with either of us. My children were grateful to have someone who knew the situation but wasn't going to get upset about it like Mum did. I still don't know what they said, but I am grateful to know that they did. I know this by such comments as "Yes, I talked that through with Stuart [family friend]" or "Grandma said there was no need to worry about that as well".

Most children, when they have problems, go to their parents and tell them all about it. When I ask children at school "What is a family?" one of the things they say is, "People you can tell everything to." Divorce can change that because although children may want to talk about how they are feeling with their parents, they are not yet adults and cannot cope with the strength and depth of their parents' hurt, anger or resentment. It is way too easy for either of the parents involved to use the conversations with their children as a way of justifying their position, or repeating old resentments, or expressing their anger and grief at what has happened. This doesn't help the child. Adult feelings are too much for them; they are children.

From my own experience I can say it is almost impossible to talk rationally about the separation in the early stages, because you haven't yet rationalized it for yourself. So suddenly the child can't tell their mother that they are angry with their father, because she is too, and it just sets off an even worse storm of resentment and emotion. Nor can they tell their father that they feel betrayed by their mother, because he is feeling betrayed too. The children are already feeling all at sea with the tensions, arguments and resentments coming from their parents, and talking to people who are also emotional about it just makes it ten times worse. When I asked teenagers who they talked to, they said, "My friends and family friends." They have chosen to talk to someone who is sympathetic but not too directly involved.

Know when the problem is serious.

Most children just want reassurance when they talk to you, or clarification about what's actually going to happen in their lives. Older children and teenagers may need to work through their own anger, grief, loss and frustration in a safe environment. Very few children of divorcees need specialist help, but some do. If a child lets you know about something serious, it needs to be passed on so they can get some professional help. Issues of violence and emotional or sexual abuse may seem "normal" to a child if this has been part of their experience for as long as they can remember, but these issues need specialist counselling if the child is to recover well. If the child is self-harming or the doctor says they are clinically depressed, then more professional help will be needed. Most schools have counsellors. However, one girl said to me, "I'd never go to see the school counsellor if I was upset – everyone would think I was pregnant!" Doctors and schools usually know where the child can find discreet, private and generally free professional help.

WHAT'S NORMAL?

> *"Were we a talking family before? I can't really remember… from the age of ten to fifteen I don't feel that I had anyone to talk to… but it's also the age when you think talking's not important."*

It made me feel sad when Rachel said that to me – sad that she felt there were no adults around for her. But there again, as she said, not every child wants to talk about their emotions at that age. They are all so different and we need to be sensitive to what the child wants. Were you "a talking family"? What's normal for you? What's normal for them? If you were "a talking family" before, then the children will probably keep on talking about their feelings to Mum or Dad or both, but if you weren't, then it would be odd to start trying to force it. Some children in the same family are natural talkers, and some don't feel the need for it. It's just their personality. It really depends on the individual child and the closeness of the relationship you've had with them before the split. Very often children will not open up to a direct question anyway.

As mentioned earlier, conversations, especially with teenagers, tend to start when they are doing something else alongside you. If they know you are available to listen, then they'll choose when they want to come and talk. One of my daughters used to wait until I'd gone to bed and the house was quiet. Then she'd come up to my room at about midnight – "Are you still awake?" – fling herself on the end of my bed, and start pouring her heart out. Sometimes I just wanted to sleep or to finish the chapter of the book I was reading, but at the same time I was touched and pleased that she still wanted to talk to me about things. And, after all, good listening doesn't require much response: just the odd nod or grunt of acknowledgment. Even I could manage that at midnight!

Then there's the age of the child to be taken into account. Young children might talk about it all in a matter-of-fact way and without much emotion and then get on with the next thing. It can seem almost heartless to us adults, but that is just the stage they are at. Older children could show more signs of worry or grief and need reassurance and to feel they are being looked after, but tears and tantrums again are normal.

GIRLS ARE DIFFERENT FROM BOYS

I think it's worth remembering at this point that boys and girls are different. They are different in their need to talk and in the way they talk. Having had two of each I am convinced it's not just personality differences in the way they communicate, but gender differences. I used to worry that I hadn't established a proper relationship with my teenage son. How could he talk to me about deep and meaningful issues if we couldn't even hold a conversation about ordinary things? I'll give you an example of one of the best of our conversations at the time.

"Did you have a good day at school, dear?"

"Yeah."

"Have you got a lot of homework?"

"Nah."

"Really? Wasn't there any set tonight?"

"Dunnit."

"Where are you going?"

"Jack's."

"When will you be back?"

"Later."

"What's on tonight, then?"

"Football."

"Will you be late?"

"Nah."

I agonized about this style of conversation for months. What sort of dreadful parent was I that my son couldn't communicate with me? He always *used* to talk. The divorce had sent him monosyllabic! He must be totally depressed about it; did he need counselling? But then I came to realize that this was an entirely normal conversation for Boys at a Certain Age. It helps here to have some friends with sons of the same age, but if you don't believe me, listen to a teenage boy arranging to meet a friend on the phone:

"Steve. Out tonight? Yeah. Bezza's. Seven. Cheers, mate. Bye."

The whole exchange takes less than thirty seconds. This is all quite normal. They go through a monosyllabic stage. They grow out of it.

This is what I mean by gender differences. Take the thirty-second exchange above. The same boy's sister will take at least an hour and a half on the phone to make a similar arrangement. This will include three possible venues, two agreed times and then a change of mind again. An in-depth discussion of what sort of thing everyone will be wearing is more or less compulsory; and then there'll be a long negotiation about which of them is going to wear that state-of-the-art-fashion, funky top they *both* bought in the same colour. Whoever wins that exchange will follow it up with a fulsome offer to lend her own jewellery, accessories and make-up to the other in compensation. This will all be interwoven with the latest school gossip, a detailed update on who's going out with whom and who's not speaking to whom any more, and how that has changed in the last hour since they got off the school bus. Somewhere between half and three-quarters of an hour after the conversation has started, there will be a loud exclamation of "Mum! Stop listening to my private conversation!" from one side or the other, and then a fifteen-minute discussion of how unreasonable parents can be and how they don't trust you. The venue and time of meeting will then be discussed and changed again. Two other friends are usually brought into the plan about now via text or Facebook and finally, finally, after at least an hour, it'll all be settled – they now all know whose house they are going to meet at to get ready before they decide where they are going.

This is all quite normal. If a female teenager wants to talk and chooses you to listen, it could take some time, the conversation will range far and wide, and it will include gossip and strong emotional opinions and feelings that are very real on that day but might not be so important tomorrow. Apart from patience, the thing you need most when listening to teenage girls is a large pinch of salt. "I hate you!", "I hate her!", "I'm never going to speak to him again!" are ways of letting off steam and neutralizing the emotions of the moment, but they don't always mean what they say. They are expressing their feelings, and it helps if you can acknowledge that feeling rather than trying to make it go away. Strangely, denying or ignoring the feeling, saying "Don't be so angry!" or "You don't really mean that!", is likely to make the child more upset and more insistent, and the whole the situation will quickly escalate.

The most comforting thing to do, surprisingly, is to acknowledge the feeling and show you recognize what they are going through – "I can see you are really cross with Dad at the moment" or "I can see you are angry about the situation". If they believe you – and it's hard not to sound patronizing – the anger and emotion will diffuse and the sadness will become a little easier to bear, because you have acknowledged and understood it. Children are less used to strong emotions than we are, so they find it hard even to understand themselves what they are feeling. By saying "I can see you are really sad about it today" you are helping the child understand the feelings they are experiencing, and that makes their confusion better. Something magical can happen if you keep your own opinions and views out of the conversation. By acknowledging the feeling and saying very little, it often gives the child space to work it out for themselves. Questioning can add to the confusion because they can't even deal with what's in front of them, but sympathetic listening with the odd "Mmm" or "Yes" or "I see" thrown in gives them the chance to put their feelings into words for themselves.

This way of helping is useful when it comes to emotions. Very often, young children are feeling things very strongly but don't know what they are feeling. A question such as: "Were you feeling angry when Daddy went home on Saturday?" will give them the opportunity to name and recognize their emotions. "Yes. I was really angry because he left!" or "No… I wasn't angry, just really sad". Giving names to their emotions like this can help them understand what they are feeling.

Actually, as discussed above, often all you need is a sympathetic silence. Many of my friends who have listened to me for ages on the phone have said, "I wish there was something I could do," and I used to say, "You just have." It is just such a relief to be able to say it all to someone who is sympathetic, really listening and trying to understand. Men in particular can feel that they are doing nothing if they are just listening. They feel at a loss with all the information, and caring dads instinctively want to find or suggest an immediate solution. "But I didn't do anything. I didn't help!" they say, but the listening itself without any advice or solution *is* the help.

Women, on the other hand, are generally much more used to talking. Ideas and connections and anecdotes and stories of our friends in similar situations fly through our minds and out of our mouths. For us it is much harder to just listen, to keep our views and emotions and the documentary we saw out of it.

There are times to talk all about it and there are times to problem-solve, but sometimes a child just wants someone who will listen.

SOMEONE TO LISTEN TO YOU

Good listening helps children recognize their emotions, but it is far more confusing if they have to deal with your emotions as well. Even teenagers cannot understand the depth of adult emotions and aren't equipped for dealing with them. I worry when I see single parents squeezing their ten-year-old to them and saying, "We're best friends. We tell each other everything." Should a child be burdened with that? I have known children at twelve or fourteen weighed down with the intimate details of their parents' sex lives or being told by grandparents, at length, all the reasons why they thought the child's parents should never have got married. All these things need to be sorted out in the minds of the family that are touched by the separation.

In order to be a good listener to children, the listeners need someone to listen to them. I certainly found as a parent that I needed to have other people to listen to *me*. I had a counsellor who listened to me and helped me sort out the confusion in my own head, and I had many friends who did the same over the phone or a coffee. Once I'd got my emotions and confusion sorted out, I found I had space to listen to my children's.

Paying for a counsellor can seem like an extravagant expense at a time when things are usually difficult financially, and yet it is really disturbing for children, even teenagers, to hear their parent's problems and to be a recipient of the burden of their emotions. Divorce is known to be one of the most stressful things any human being can go through. Emotional support of the parents during divorce is really important for the children. Studies have shown that long term (after six years) the children who have adjusted well and show few adverse effects from the divorce of their parents are those whose parents themselves have adjusted well and come to terms with the new arrangements.[2] Counsellors are not advice-givers but skilled listeners (for more on this, see Chapter 10: "Looking After the Parents").

IT'S NEVER TOO LATE TO TALK

"It's left me with issues about trust and more cynical... If Luke [her partner] says, 'I'm not going to leave you... I'm not like him,' I think, 'Yeah, like anything's forever.' I've less trust in men; I keep thinking he's going to cheat on me some day," said Rachel to me recently. She also said, "But Grandma says it doesn't do you any good to hang on to grudges and resentments; you've just got to let them go. I think she's right. I don't want to be a cynical person." Even now, fifteen years after her parents split up, her adult self is processing it and her grandma is still listening.

It made me wonder if all grandmas say things like this, because just yesterday my friend Joanne said the turning point for her son was when *his* grandma, who'd been listening and allowing him to talk about how he felt for who knows how many years, pointed out that if his mum could forgive his dad, then surely he could. The son, then twenty-seven, drove to the family home they had all left twelve years earlier, and said he felt like driving his car down the drive and straight into the lounge because he was still so angry that other people were living there and not their old family. But instead, he just collapsed over the steering wheel and sobbed and sobbed. For him, this was a turning point. It's good to let all the hurt out, even if it's years after the event. Grief has a habit of taking you unawares. A sight, a sound, an anniversary or a memory can trigger it quite unexpectedly and some effects can linger for a long time. I'm not suggesting this is the way to advise everyone or that grandparents should pester their poor grandchildren with the concept of forgiveness to help them get better. I just offer these two real-life examples of the positive effects that a trusting relationship and someone to talk things over with can have.

LISTENING IN SHORT

Good listening is:

- showing you are listening;

- naming their emotions;

- rephrasing what they have just said;

- accepting their feelings;

- leaving space for them to work out their solution;

- allowing others to listen to your child too.

Good listening is not:

- interrupting;

- giving them advice;

- saying what you think;

- questioning;

- having a conversation;

- having them listen to you.

6

Loving
· · · · · · · · · · ·

"Make sure [the children] know they're loved."
(G12)

Everyone wants to be loved. If children feel unloved they feel empty inside and may try to fill that gap with other sorts of attention-seeking behaviour. Little ones try temper tantrums and sometimes refuse to eat, or regress to carrying their teddy or blankie around again or sucking their thumb. Teenagers may try bad behaviour or drink or sex to fill the gaps. (Or they might just be being teenagers.) One of the commonest problems reported by the teenagers in my survey was loneliness or a feeling of isolation. It is as if there is so much going on between their parents that they feel their needs are lost. They don't feel loved.

When your family is breaking up, there is a loss of trust in the people you have trusted most in the world. Trust is a key element of love. It's not that parents have stopped loving their children and it's not that they've forgotten about their needs; it's just that there are so many other enormous drains on the adults' emotional and physical energies that there is nothing left over.

As I was writing Chapter 3 about organization it seemed daft to me that we never made a better financial arrangement for our children than what boiled down to "I'll look after these two and you look after those two". From this distance it seems ridiculous, and yet I know that it was the best arrangement we could agree on at the time. If we just consider the finances, though, there is so much that comes under that heading that has to be sorted out between the adults. How are the assets divided? Who will look after the debts? What arrangements can be made for pensions? How is the business divided? Who's paying for the divorce? Will the house have to be sold or can one partner buy the other out? Any detail of any of this can blow up into a long drawn-out and expensive disagreement, and somehow the idea of exactly where Johnny gets his pocket money from is lost among the bigger problems. It is just an illustration of how the children's needs can easily get left behind, even though the courts and everyone involved are trying to put them first. The children pick this up. Their frequent references to feeling "lonely" or "isolated" are, I think, a reaction to the preoccupation of both their parents in sorting out what is a painful situation for all.

It has been a real revelation for me to realize that people receive love or praise or thanks in different ways. If you invited people for dinner, some would say "thank you" effusively for the meal; some would eat it all up with great gusto and leave a clean plate; some would say thanks as they left in the midst of the goodbye hug; some would have said thanks in advance with a bunch of flowers or bottle of wine; others would do the washing-up in appreciation. Which of those actions would make you feel they had really appreciated the meal? I always think that it shows your appreciation if you bring a small gift with you. But my mother-in-law, a great cook, wouldn't care whether or not her guests brought a gift with them; she talks with great pleasure of the people she has invited for meals who have cleared their plates and asked for more. To her that was the proof they had enjoyed it – actions. My friend Jean doesn't mind if you leave food (people's appetites are different) but very much appreciates a word of thanks.

Some children need hugs and touch for reassurance. Some want gifts. Some want you to do something nice for them like go out for the day. And some want just to be with you – time spent in your company is important to them. Say you'd arranged an evening out with your child and the plan had gone wrong. You couldn't get tickets to the game after all. Depending on how they feel loved, the children's reaction will be different and the solution to the problem will be different as well. If they thought you were giving them a gift, then replace it with an equally good gift – in this case, "I've rearranged it for next week and we've got better seats" would make your child feel loved. But if it was your time and attention they wanted, they might feel they weren't loved. So offering "Would you like to come round anyway and we could watch something on TV?" or "So we're going out to Pizza Hut instead" might be just as good as going to the match.

THE FIVE LOVES

I have found Gary Chapman's series on the "five love languages" really helpful in my relationships with my own four children.[1] He points out that love is given and received in five main ways: by the words "I love you", by spending time with the person you love, by giving gifts, by doing things for the other person, and by physical touch. What revolutionized my own relationship with my children was realizing that everyone majors in one or two of those ways. That is the way they want to be loved; in fact, they don't feel loved unless you communicate love in that way. The problem is that we tend to give love in the way that makes most sense to us. But it might not communicate love to our children if they are speaking a different "love language". The way I prefer to receive love may not be the way they do. And it is usual for people to give love in the way they prefer to receive it.

Gifts

If any of my children came in from school obviously upset, throwing their schoolbag around in a temper, my immediate reaction would be to put my arms around them, give them a big hug, and say, "I can see you've had a bad day. Wanna talk?" This always worked with one of my daughters, who would hug me back or cry on my shoulder for a bit, and then start to pour out her problems. I (on a good day) would listen, and half an hour later she'd feel better. So imagine my confusion when my *other* daughter hit the same stage. *Bang!* goes the door as she comes in from school. *Crash!* goes the bag against the skirting board. "Mutter, mutter, swear" as the coat misses the coat stand. I know these signs. It has not been a good day.

I swing into action, arms outstretched, and wrap her in a hug. She goes rigid in my arms and pushes me away, "Get off!" she yells and goes storming upstairs to her room.

"I was just trying to show some sympathy," I think (and sometimes yell) to her retreating back. But she takes no notice. I try again. I go upstairs, put my head round the door, and with my best sympathetic voice say, "Wanna talk about it?"

"No! Go away! Leave me alone."

If we were lucky she'd come down when dinner was ready, eat half of it and retreat as soon as possible. I was left feeling like an awful mother whose daughter didn't want to talk to her and didn't even realize that I loved her. Was there a deeper problem or damage that I had missed? Why was she behaving like this? What I'd missed was that she received love in a different way from her sister. I'd read about this stuff but thought it must be exaggerated. It never occurred to me that she might not *want* to be hugged at that time or to *spend time* with her mum getting over it, because that's what I wanted at the same age and in the same situation. However, when I tried what I thought was "normal" it just made things worse, and often would escalate horribly quickly into a real argument between us. I began to leave her alone. I felt useless. I was worried about our relationship. Had our time apart damaged it so much?

Then one day I allowed myself a couple of "what ifs". What if this love language stuff was right? What if she really didn't see hugs and the offer of quality time as me loving her? When did she usually look happy? When I gave her something. How did she usually show she loved me ... by helping. She was always saying, "I've done the washing-up", "I've cleaned the bathroom" and "I've tidied my room." So what if her primary way of showing and receiving love was by doing things for other people or by giving and receiving gifts? I was sceptical. It wouldn't work for me, but maybe she wanted to be loved in a different way.

Teenage years are turbulent and it wasn't long before something else brought an angry stomping teenager back to me. I'd given up trying to hug her. Off she went to her room as usual and all my helplessness kicked in again. I'd nothing left to lose so I racked my brains to try to think of what I could give her that she'd like (and wouldn't be expensive!). My whole system baulked at the idea of giving a reward for "bad" behaviour, but then I reminded myself that I wasn't trying to reward her behaviour but show her I cared. What could I do for her that would help? So I went to the corner shop and bought her a small packet of penny sweets that I knew she'd liked as a little girl. I got her favourite pizza out of the freezer to cook for her tea. It was all I could think of. Then I took a deep breath and a cup of tea up to her room.

I put the tea and the sweets on her bedside table without touching her and said, "I could see you were upset so I got these to cheer you up... and I'm cooking pizza for tea as it's your favourite." Then I started out of the room before I got the backlash. But to my astonishment she seemed really touched.

"Oh thanks, Mum!" she said. "I'll be down to help in a minute. I'm just a bit upset at the moment – Hannah was horrible to me." I couldn't believe it.

If your child feels loved when they receive gifts, then it might not matter to them if you can't come to their birthday party but it would matter if you didn't send them a present. For day-to-day showing you care, try gifts. They don't have to be expensive; sometimes I bought my daughter a single gerbera on the way home from work or shopping. When she was little she loved Kinder eggs – you get chocolate *and* a present. Have a bag full of inexpensive presents that your child could choose from when they see you; or you could send an interesting card with "Happy Monday" on it.

Some of the people who saw the anonymous results of the survey were shocked that "you get twice as many Christmas presents" came up as one of the advantages of divorce. But I don't think it was *just* because children are all mercenary little things; I think some children genuinely feel more loved when they get a gift.

Quality time
However, if the child's primary love language isn't gifts, all the sweets, cups of coffee, outings, iPads and Porsches in the world won't make them feel loved; it may be that their primary love language is quality time, or one of the others.

Ian's story
Last week a friend was telling me about his fifteen-year-old daughter who had been discouraged all her life from seeing him by her mother. They managed to spend a day together and he was full of ideas about where they could go and what they could do, but she wasn't excited about any of it. In the end she said, "Dad, I just want to talk to you and get to know you." So that's what they did. How precious is that! He didn't realize how rare a remark from a teenager that was. It's normal for teenagers to almost see it as their *duty* to avoid socializing with their parents. But she wanted to see him. Just to talk. She just wanted some quality time with her dad.

Quality time doesn't have to be lots of time: it just means whatever time you have with your child, make it count. It also means that if time and attention really matter to your child, then missing a date you have fixed with them, even for a good reason, will be very hard for them.

So for adults trying to help youngsters through their parents' divorce, here are some of the children's ideas:

> *"Tell them they're always welcome at your house."*
> *(G15)*

> *"Spend more time with them; have a long*
> *conversation every once in a while." (B14)*

> *"Just be available in case they want to [come] over*
> *for lunch etc." (G14)*

> *"Tell them they can spend time after school at [your]*
> *house." (B13)*

> *"Ask them if they want to come round and talk."*
> *(G15)*

All these ideas ask for you to be there with them. These pupils are saying that time with people who love them helps.

Words of love

For some children, reassurance that they are loved doesn't stick in their minds unless they have it in words. They need to hear you say it to their face, in writing or on the phone. They don't really believe you love them in their heart of hearts otherwise. I'm reminded of that famous song from *Fiddler on the Roof* when Tevye asks his wife Golde if she loves him. Golde gives and receives love via acts of service; everything she's ever done for him bears evidence to that fact. But Tevye is only really content when he hears the words "I love you" from her.

In the following quotes from the survey, both male and female teenagers are asking for *words*. The emphasis is on "tell them".

> *"Remind [the children] how much they're loved and explain that [divorce] is the best option." (G15)*

> *"Tell them that it is not their fault, and there is nothing they can do to change it. Tell them in the end the family will be happier." (G14)*

> *"Comfort them; tell them [that the parents] are happier now the divorce [has happened]." (G14)*

> *"Tell them they love them." (G14)*

> *"Talk to them and see how they feel." (B13)*

Actions speak louder than words

My mum used to get a huge glossy card from her mother every year on her birthday, with a long poem all about what a wonderful daughter she was, but it never made her feel loved. "If she loves me that much, why hasn't she phoned?" she'd say. "When did she last come round to see us?" For Mum, actions spoke louder than words. She used to love the *Fiddler on the Roof* song. I think she identified with Golde – it was so obvious to her that if you loved people, you did things for them.

If actions speak louder than words to your child, then saying "Mummy and Daddy will still love you" might not reassure them. Gifts might not make them feel wanted, but what you do (or don't do) for them will make a big difference to them understanding that you love them. If your child puts a lot of store by what you do for them, they will feel really loved if you sit down to help them with their homework or tests. If you are happy to drive them to their music lessons or sports clubs, it will also help them feel loved – they know you are busy and just doing it for them. Make their bedtime drink just the way they like it or cook their favourite meal. If they are ill, finding them a good DVD to watch or making chicken soup will make them feel more loved than stroking them or sounding sympathetic.

Here is a selection of the things children say will help in that very difficult phase of confusion around the divorce (which can go on for months and years). They are all things you can *do* for them to make it easier.

> *"Make sure your child gets to see both parents regularly." (B14)*

> *"Argue when the children aren't around." (B14)*

> *"Do the divorce quickly and get it out of the way." (B13)*

> *"Let them stay with grandparents to get away from the havoc." (G13)*

Do actions always speak louder than words? This is certainly true for some, but maybe not all.

Touch
Two of my four children want only one response when they are hurting or feeling vulnerable: a big hug. That's great as far as I'm concerned because that makes me feel better too. Every morning my (second) husband gives me a kiss, a hug, and a cup of coffee. I like the cup of coffee but it wouldn't bother me to go down and make it myself – I'd still feel loved. But if I didn't

have the kiss and hug, I'd feel unloved. Other people could do without the hug as long as they got the coffee.

Some families are not hugging families and some people nowadays are so conscious of the risks of child safety in their jobs that they filter touch out of their lives.

If touch is important to your child, here are some ways to get more touch into their world, making them feel more loved and secure even if their family circumstances are changing.

Younger children

Hug and kiss your children on leaving for school and coming home. Make it part of the normal greeting. With younger children, sit them on your knee when reading bedtime stories. Play counting or singing games that have lots of actions and touch such as "Pat-a-cake, pat-a-cake" or "This Little Piggy". Snuggle up on the sofa if watching TV together. Hold hands when you are out shopping. Buy a soft and cuddly toy or blanket for them. Make sure you remember their special toy or "snuggly" and take care that it doesn't get lost between houses.

Older children

They might feel they are "growing out of" kisses, so pat them on the back or high five them if they've done something good (that probably works better in the States). Tickle them if they like it. Play rough and tumble games with them. Give a quick touch on their arm as well as using words to show you are concerned about them. Play contact sports with them and make the most of goal celebrations.

In the words of the children:

"Make them feel loved, give them hugs!" (G13)

"First chat about being there if they want to talk or [have] a hug." (B15)

WHICH IS THE MOST IMPORTANT?

So how can you tell which of the five ways of giving and receiving love are the most important to your child? How can you reassure your child or grandchild that they are still loved? You can start by observing the way they give love. Do they come up to you and hug you when you meet? Then it's likely they feel loved if hugged.

Do they offer you their teddy when you are sad? Do they say things such as "I've tidied my bedroom, Dad" or "I've done the washing-up"? If so, actions communicate love to them.

Do they always remember to get you something on Mother's Day? Do they give you their paintings when they've done them? Pick you a bunch of daisies from the lawn? Give you their last Rolo? If so, then they will feel loved when they are given gifts.

Do they want to be with you when you are washing up/doing the gardening/working from home? Do they phone when you are away? Yes? Then they love sharing quality time with you. They probably want your time and attention back.

Children usually give love in the way they would like to receive it. If you're not sure, then try offering a choice and see if it makes a difference. For example, "Would you like to spend Saturday afternoon making cakes with me [quality time] or shall I drive you to the stables for a horse riding lesson [helpful action]?" "I can see you're upset: would you like a hug [touch] or a cup of tea and a biscuit [action]?" "What do you want for your birthday? A bicycle [gift] or a day out at the adventure park with me [quality time]?"

With young children, you could ask questions whenever the subject comes up. For instance, if a child says, "Grandma doesn't love me any more" ask, "What would make you think she did love you?" The answer could be: "She'd give me a cuddle/remember my birthday/come and see me/take me out for the day/finish mending my bike." Again, this will give you an idea of how they receive love. If you are watching a film together, ask questions: "How do you know that the daddy in the film loves his children?" You might be surprised at the answer you get. Or just experiment. I experimented with my daughter when she didn't want my hugs and was amazed by the difference it made just bringing a little gift. Try something different and see if it improves your relationship with your children and their feeling that they are safe in your love.

LOVING AT A DISTANCE

I found it very difficult to be apart from my girls for so long as they were growing up. It felt as if I didn't know them. When my daughter Rachel was eleven, I knew she was into her sports fashion phase and loved the trainers, tracksuits, T-shirts and hats with the "right" names on and the "right" number of stripes down the sides for that season. So there I was standing in the "right" sports shop surrounded by a warehouse full of trendy sports fashion items and I had no idea what to buy her. I knew her size and I knew the colours she preferred but I just didn't know what to get her. What did she already have? The helpful young shop assistant said brightly, "We can hold it for you. Why don't you check her wardrobe tonight and see what she's got, and come back tomorrow if it's right?" She then looked very surprised as I had to leave rapidly to hide my tears. For the first time in eleven years I couldn't just "check her wardrobe".

Similarly, I knew it was important for Abigail that I came to her parents' evening and showed interest in her progress at school and yet I was not always informed of the things that were going on. If this can happen to a parent living in the same town as her children, how much worse is it for parents separated by hundreds of miles or even living in other countries? Grandparents, aunties and uncles want to show their concern too. This is even more complicated if you belong to the "other" side of the family, the one that is the visiting parent rather than the one who has the main home. It may not be easy to stay in contact with your grandchild or nephew if their mother or father doesn't want to encourage contact from the family of their ex. If so, how do you stay in touch and show your love at a distance? It depends in part on how the child likes to be loved. If they appreciate words, you can email regularly. Send cards to celebrate all the important occasions you can and write how proud you are of them. Text them. Give as many words of praise, encouragement and love as you can. When you do see the child, *say* how much you are pleased to see them and *tell* them you love them.

If they feel loved when you spend time with them, don't worry. Your time with them may be limited but interestingly children report that although they may not see their parent as often as they did before, they feel they can have a better relationship with them as the time they spend is concentrated on them. It is the quality of the time that counts, not the amount. Plan your time together and ask the child what they would like to do. Make time to phone them regularly if you can't be with them. I coped with the fact that I had lost my day-to-day contact with my girls by comparing my situation to parents who had children at boarding school. All over the world children go to school away from their parents and maintain good and loving relationships with them. Make the time you do have together count – don't bring work home that weekend.

If it's gifts that show them they are loved, then it will be important to remember birthdays and Christmas and to make sure the gift arrives on time. You could send a random present every now and then; it doesn't have to be expensive. Celebrate a good report or a sporting achievement or a music exam passed well with a small gift. Put money regularly into a "college fund" or "computer fund". These things will really count.

If the children need to see your actions to feel loved, then it will be important to them that you keep any promises you make. Always turn up on time and without fuss if an arrangement has been made. Have a Plan B if something comes up at work, so you can still go to their match or see the play they are in.

If your child likes lots of hugs and touch, they will miss you when you are away from them and can't touch them, but "touch" as a sense is still important to them. So they will appreciate any soft, cuddly toys and clothes you give them. Greet your child with a hug and a kiss when you do see them. Pick them up and cuddle them, tickle and use rough and tumble, put your arm round them.

Despite wanting our children to feel loved and secure, we know that we are all going to make mistakes. There will be times when we let them down and they are, rightly, cross with us. It's at those times that the little known art of apology can help. Apologies mend relationships, but only if they are believed and accepted by the other person.

One way to mend a relationship with your child when something has gone wrong is to apologize in a way they can "hear". Those five methods work for apology as well as love.[2] For example, say you miss a child's birthday and their present arrives late. If they are a "wordy" person, then make sure you phone or write a card and say clearly that you are sorry you didn't get their present to them on time. It'll make all the difference. If they like gifts, then send them an extra present or accessory to the present to say sorry. If they want time with you, make time for a long phone call or an extra visit. If they are at your home, do something with them. If actions speak to them, show them the system you've put in place to make sure it doesn't happen again. And then make sure it *doesn't* happen again. If touch speaks to them, give them a hug in addition to telling them you're sorry and you'll find the apology is much more readily accepted.

A late present is a simple example of something that may have been your fault (you were too busy to remember the date) or may not have been (you allowed enough time but the post was late again). In a family break-up, there are far more serious mistakes we make that are sometimes our fault and sometimes unavoidable. How many of us could be strong enough to say "I'm sorry I was rude about your mother. I shouldn't have said what I did. I know it upset you"? Or "I'm sorry I insisted you come and live with me. I wanted you to very much, but I know it would have been better if you'd stayed with Dad"? How many of us would be prepared, even years later, to say "I'm sorry I hurt you" and take our responsibility for that hurt? Apologies cannot change the past but they can heal the residual hurt that lingers and lingers. I know people in their sixties who still long to hear their parents apologize for the difficulties they caused them. If we can apologize to our children, it teaches them how to apologize themselves. Much more important than that it helps them heal, to feel truly loved, and it improves our relationship with them.

LOVING IN SHORT

It helps children to know they are loved if you:

- spend time with them;

- tell them you love them;

- give them presents;

- give them hugs;

- do the little things for them as well as the big things;

- find out how each one best receives your love/ understands you love them;

- let other people love them too;

- mend the relationship with apology when necessary.

7

Discipline

· · · · · · · · · · · · · · · ·

*"How was I supposed to have my adolescence when
you two were having yours?"*

This was the reaction of my eldest son, now grown up but
sixteen when his parents divorced. As he remembers it, he was
just getting to the point where emotional outburst, irrational
behaviour, finding out who you really are, getting drunk,
having lots of sexual encounters and all sorts of other things
on the boundaries of acceptable behaviour were considered the
norm and part of the process of adolescence. Adolescence is not
supposed to be standing on the sidelines watching your parents
go through the same. Parents are supposed to help guide and
restrain their children through this stage; Michael found his
parents more concerned with their emotions than his, with
their lives than his and with their plans for the future than his.

Maybe in the hearts of all children of divorced parents there
is that same cry, if unacknowledged. How was I supposed to
bond with you when you weren't there? How was I supposed
to have my terrible twos when you were having yours? How
was I supposed to adjust to life on my own at nursery when
you weren't adjusting to life on your own at home? How was
I supposed to work hard at school when you couldn't keep
working at your job? It is so hard for parents to deal consistently

with their children's behaviour when there is so much else occupying their thoughts.

Therefore, when you are so busy having your adolescence that you don't notice the children are having theirs – until there is a crisis – it helps to have a few ideas and short cuts that other people have found useful. There are many excellent parenting books and websites out there and there are techniques for engaging cooperation that all teachers use, consciously or unconsciously, in their work. I'm sharing some ideas here, but for more detailed information and a mass of ideas see the booklist.

SETTING BOUNDARIES

Discipline is often thought to be synonymous with punishment but the two are not interchangeable. The word "discipline" comes from the Latin word *discipulus*, which means a student or learner. We get the English word "disciple" from it, and it means someone who is taught the right path in life by their guru or mentor. Discipline is about providing a protected environment for the children so that they don't get hurt, and it's about gaining the children's cooperation so that the family and society run smoothly. We all need to learn how to behave in a group. It's the parents who teach their children what's acceptable and what is not. Discipline means setting boundaries to show children where the limits are. It is fine to dislike your food (not everyone enjoys the same things), but it's not fine to throw it on the carpet. It's acceptable to be angry, but it's not acceptable to hit your brother with your dinosaur. There must be limits if we are all to live together happily.

HELPING CHILDREN RECOGNIZE THEIR FEELINGS

It's worth remembering that what we might see as "bad behaviour" at home or at school could just be the way the child is reacting to the difficulties of the divorce. Regressing to earlier "babyish" behaviour, wanting a bottle at bedtime, coming into your bed, throwing tantrums and refusing to cooperate are all common in children of divorced parents, because these are just childlike ways of coping with the emotions they feel at the loss of their family. Showing you understand and accept their emotions goes a long way to defusing some of their bad behaviour. So the incident with the dinosaur has to be dealt with, of course, and the tears mopped up and peace restored, but alongside that it is worth a comment such as "I could see you were feeling angry". It's just a descriptive remark, not a judgmental one.

We talked about naming the emotions in the chapter on loss as a way of showing that you understand what they are feeling, but in this context I think it is more about reassurance. If you can name them, you are letting the children know that it is acceptable to have these strong emotions, and that you will still love them regardless of what they are feeling. When parents are divorcing, children feel very guilty, as we have already seen. They need lots of reassurance and lots of expressions of love.

On the other hand, excusing or tolerating bad behaviour because you know they are upset – or you are feeling guilty too about the effect the separation has had on them – won't help either of you in the long run. Letting them get away with things that they and you know are not right just confirms their fears that their parents have abandoned them. Parents may have lost their husband/wife role but they have not lost their parenting role. One of the ways you can reassure them that you are still there and you do still care is to continue to act like their parent, and that includes letting them know where the boundaries between good and bad behaviour are. If you ignore a behavioural problem it will continue until the situation escalates into one you can't ignore, undermining your parental authority.

HOUSE RULES

Every home has its own house rules, even if no one has ever written them down. My ex-husband and I never had a set of rules written down in our home either when we were together or when we were separated, but everyone knew that certain things were expected. Things such as: Children are responsible for the tidiness of their own rooms. Come to meals when called. Flush the loo when you've finished. No muddy boots in the house. Bedtime's at eight o'clock. Save sweets for after meals. Take it in turns to do the washing-up. Put your own dirty clothes in the laundry basket. If you want a lift anywhere, write it on the calendar.

We all knew what the rules were. I remember a time when "Is it on the calendar?" was an almost daily refrain in our house. When a new problem arose, a new rule or expectation was introduced. For example, when they were teenagers there was suddenly the new rule: If you're not home by six, don't expect a meal.

It may seem over-formal to actually write down and put up a set of house rules in your home, but if things are sliding into semi-chaos, the children keep needing reminders of what's expected of them. If you have started a new family with children from different families, then a written set of rules helps everyone realize you are serious about the standard of behaviour that you want.

PLAYING ONE ADULT OFF AGAINST ANOTHER

All children try to play their parents off against each other when they have been refused something by one of them. When the parents are separated, some children hone this to a very fine skill indeed, playing on their parents' guilt. You can minimize the effects of the divorce by keeping to the same routines you have had, or by starting some clear new routines so the children feel secure in what is going to happen in their daily lives. Ideally both households will have the same routines and the same house rules as each other so the children know what to expect, and know one parent will follow through on what the other has decided.

The best defence against a child trying to play one parent off against the other is a united front, at least in the way the children are to be brought up. If you have a set of house rules that you have agreed together, then you have an immediate answer to the complaint "Daddy always lets me do that!" or "Mummy says I can eat sweets before meals!".

However, I know this is an ideal and is not achievable in every case. But at least you can have clear boundaries in your own household. Children are very adaptable. If confronted with the "Mummy lets me" argument (which may or may not be true), just make your expectations clear with a matter-of-fact statement such as "Mummy decides what happens in her house, but here in my house we *do* brush our teeth before bed" or whatever.

GETTING THEM TO COOPERATE

Try giving a choice, not a command. Commands set up battles that the child then wants to win. "Get your coat on now!" is a signal for a battle of wills. But "Would you like to put your coat on yourself or have me help you?" or "Are you going to put your coat on now or in five minutes when your programme has finished?" puts the power in their hands and gets their cooperation. The key here is to select two things that you genuinely don't mind them choosing. In the above scenario either of the choices will be fine. "Would you like to put your coat on or go out in the snow without it?" is not a realistic choice; you will not be able to follow through on the latter if they choose it. My mum would say to me, "Never threaten anything unless you are prepared to actually do it." It's really good advice. It is so important to follow through on any threats, or the children will start to take no notice of them because they know you don't mean them. If, like me, you have found yourself about to threaten something that you are not prepared to do, then turn the threat into a description of your feelings. You may start to say, "If you don't put your toys away you're going to bed with no tea," but unless you are prepared to follow through, rescue the threat mid-sentence with an innocuous ending such as: "If you don't put your toys away... you're going to have a cross mummy." (True!) Empty threats never get cooperation from a child.

Another way of getting their cooperation is to start what you want to say to them with "I" rather than "You". Such as "I am annoyed with you" rather than "*You* are annoying!" In that way you tell the child that it's the behaviour that is wrong, not them – "I'm hurt that you said that" rather than "You rude boy!". It's a subtle difference but it makes it clear that it's not them you are rejecting but that particular behaviour. I have found in teaching that if you label a child enough times "You're so naughty!" they will live up to the label. Why would they expect good behaviour of themselves if everyone they meet is telling them they are naughty? "You're so naughty!" just reinforces a negative picture of themselves.

ROUTINE

Often the battle of wills is around a particular issue or time, such as getting up in the morning, going to bed and staying in bed, going round the supermarket or having a tantrum about being strapped into a car seat. The good news here is that thousands of other parents have had the same problems. And that means that there are tried and tested routines out there in parenting books and websites that really do work (for example, www.supernanny.co.uk; www.Mumsnet.co.uk). Toilet training, bedtime and shopping routines can all make life much more bearable with toddlers and young children. These issues are no different for the children of divorced parents than for the children of any parent. The difference is that a divorced parent is more likely not to have back-up from another adult. Also, the parent is likely to be more preoccupied or stressed with the other difficulties going on in their lives.

REWARDS AND PRAISE

Praise is powerful. If you can find *anything* to praise, then praise it and you will be surprised at the difference it will make. "I asked you to tidy your room" is more effective than "You are so lazy you can't even tidy your own room", but even better is "You've made a start on your room already. Well done".

If you suspect that their bad behaviour is because they want more attention from you, then try to catch them out doing something right rather than something wrong: "You two have been playing so well today [big hug]" or "Thank you for tidying your toys up before I'd even asked".

With little children, a reward chart might help. Put a sticker on every time they do something well. Children love stickers. There are several reward charts available to buy or download. Reward charts work well when the reward is something the children want (a trip out, a new item of clothing or toy) and as long as it is not too easy to earn, or else it will lose its value (twenty-five stickers, not three).

I would like now to put in a plea for exhausted mums and dads all over the country. It takes the patience of a saint and the self-control of a Tibetan monk to do some of the things I have just mentioned. Shouting, screaming, slapping, threatening punishment and getting into a temper are far easier than biting your tongue (again), answering in an adult way and looking for the best in a very annoying situation. So why not have your own star chart?

ALTERNATIVES TO PUNISHMENT

Dr Haim Ginott, the noted child psychologist, pioneered a series of skills that work as an alternative to punishment. He pointed out the fact that in most cases punishment doesn't work, at least in the sense that it doesn't change the children's behaviour for the better. It leaves them thinking, "I'll get back at them for that," rather than, "How can I put that right?" Take throwing food around at mealtimes; say my four-year-old habitually likes to throw her food on the floor when she doesn't want it. If I react immediately with "You bad girl!" and give her a punishment – "Straight to your room!" or "No sweets for you now!" – she has taken in two distinct messages:

I am a bad person.
Mummy doesn't like me.

That's why next time she throws the food she's just living up to the picture she already has of herself. "I'm a bad person, therefore I'm the sort that throws food and doesn't do what Mum wants." If she doesn't want the punishment again she may modify her behaviour a bit, but the behaviour won't change. On the next occasion she may wait until your back is turned before she throws the food, but she'll still throw it. If you don't notice, she gets the feeling "I got one back at Mummy!" If you do notice, she gets a shocked reaction from you: "Rosie! You're throwing food again." These are both nice *positive* feelings. Even the negative reaction from you is a positive thing for her as it shows she has the power to control you. This effect is multiplied if there are friends or siblings at the table to witness it and laugh.

Positive feelings go a long way to reinforcing unacceptable behaviour. These are such positive feelings that she may even do it in front of you again and think the punishment a reasonable pay-off for the attention she's getting from you and other people. To get round this, Dr Ginott suggests a number of possible alternatives to the immediate reaction of bad behaviour = punishment. Instead of saying, "Bad girl! Go to your room" you could try:

1. Showing you disapprove of the behaviour, not the person
So, in the above example: "Rosie! Throwing food is messy and stains the carpet" is criticizing the action, not her, and is preferable to "Rosie! *You* are a bad girl".

2. Stating your expectations
It's not always obvious to children what is expected. "Rosie! You threw your food on the floor when you were in your high chair but you are big enough to sit at the table now. We don't throw food in the dining room" shows her what is expected and says you are expecting her to be able to behave in a more mature way.

3. Showing the child how to put things right
For example, "The dustpan and brush are over there. Sweep it up and put it in the bin." This works well as a statement on its own, or could be linked with the above.

4. Giving a choice
"Either pick that up or eat your dinner on your own tomorrow." Here, eating the dinner on her own is a punishment but it is not one you have given her; it is one she chooses to accept or not. This distinction may seem pedantic, but actually it's giving the responsibility to her to choose to modify her behaviour or to take the consequences of her own bad behaviour. You don't dictate the punishment: she chooses whether she'd rather put it right now or take the exclusion tomorrow.

5. *Allowing the child to experience the consequences of their behaviour*

In this case you could just refuse to clear up anything she drops. Admittedly this is a lot easier if it's on a tiled or vinyl floor, but when Rosie returns at tea time to sit among the food she threw at breakfast and lunch maybe she'll appreciate the consequences of what she's doing. This is really hard! It worked well for me over the washing. No clothes were washed in our house unless the children put them in the laundry basket. The most famous example of this technique is Jessica Tyler, who found international renown after she blogged about going on strike to show her daughters the consequences of their behaviour.

6. *Expressing how you feel, but focusing on the problem*

When we are angry and want to express how we feel, it often turns into a judgmental rant or lecture, such as: "You are such a naughty girl [judgment]. This is the third time this week I've had to speak to you about this. Don't you take any notice of anything I say? It's in one ear and out the other with you; I don't know why I bother with you [lecture]."

Instead of this, try expressing how you feel: "I am not happy about all this food on the floor." Focus on the problem: "It'll get trodden into the carpet and be really difficult to clear up. People usually get a floor-cloth when they make a mess like that."

7. *Problem-solving together*

This alternative takes time, which is not usually available on the spur of the moment, but it works well for an ongoing problem. Using this technique helps you stay calm. Ask the child four key questions:

What have you just done?
What problem has that made for other people?
What problem has it made for you?
What are you going to do about it?

The important thing here is that you spend some time very calmly talking about it. The adult does *not* tell the child what they've done wrong or what to do about it; they just ask the key questions and wait for the answers. The child comes up with the ideas. The most important part of the technique is asking the question "What are you going to do about it?" or "What can you do to make this situation better?" If the child then decides for themselves to pick up the mess or suggests getting the dustpan and brush, then you have succeeded together. Without raising your voice, you have gained the child's cooperation in solving the problem. The message this leaves the child with is "I am good at solving problems" and "Mummy listens to me as if I am important".

When a child's parents are separating, the child is, of course, feeling particularly insecure. Having a few alternatives to the usual "shout–punishment" way of discipline can give greater security to the child by showing them their parents do still have the boundaries they expect, while still loving them.

Dr Haim Ginott's principles are explained in more detail in the book *How to Talk So Kids Will Listen & Listen So Kids Will Talk*,[1] which does what it says in the title.

BALANCE

The parent who has primary care often feels as if they have all the disciplining and boring routines to do, while the other parent does all the "fun" things. Having been in both situations, I wonder if the problem is partly one of perception. Sulks and tantrums happen on fun days out as well as on mundane visits to the supermarket. It is important, though, if you are the main carer, to make sure you have fun times with the children as well as routine times.

On the other hand, parents who have visiting rights can feel alienated from their children and not included in their care and day-to-day life. That is why it is so necessary to show your child that you have boundaries too, even if you are only seeing them for that day. Because you want that only day or weekend you are having with them to be as pleasant as possible, there is a tendency to bend over backwards and let the child get away with things that you all know are unacceptable. If you do, they will feel you don't care. You will only reinforce the idea that you are not a real parent because the child knows that a parent is supposed to put boundaries on their behaviour. I think it's this question of where your authority comes from that makes discipline so difficult for step-parents, and that is a question we shall deal with in the next chapter.

So that brings us back to the question "How was I supposed to have my adolescence when you two were having yours?" Divorced parents may need to be a little more aware than before about what being a parent means, especially with the difficult issue of teaching boundaries or discipline. I'm glad my son was able to tell me eventually that it was difficult for him. I know he sometimes felt more adult than the adults in his life, but his father and I can't have done too bad a job as he passed all his exams, has a professional career and has turned out to be a law-abiding, confident human being. Looking back, we didn't quite realize, as he was the eldest, how his needs were changing.

Maybe, if they knew how to express it, a toddler might say: "How was I supposed to have my toddler tantrums if you two were having yours?" The next three chapters are part of that answer too. In "New Family" we look at the specific question of how best to integrate other adults into the family. In "Changes" we look at how children's needs alter as the years pass, which is something my ex-husband and I probably weren't aware of and both needed to keep an eye on. "Looking After the Parents" is relevant to this question too, because our children will take their cue from us, and if we deal with our problems by resorting to tantrums, blaming others or alcohol, they are more likely to as well.

DISCIPLINE IN SHORT

It helps children to know they have clear boundaries. So,

- help them recognize what they are feeling;

- make your expectations clear;

- to get cooperation, try problem-solving instead of ordering;

- instead of lecturing, try describing the problem;

- express your disapproval of the behaviour, not the child;

- start negative comments with "I" not "you";

- give a choice;

- allow your child to experience the consequences of their actions;

- suggest how the child could put things right;

- balance responsibilities with the other parent.

8

New Family

· · · · · · · · · · · · · · · · ·

"Don't get another partner very soon at all." (G14)

Living with people you don't know very well always takes some getting used to. Many of us have horror stories about the state of the fridge at university or the difficulties of getting bathroom-time in a flat share. As adults we know how difficult it is to share a home with strangers, so why do we think our children will readily adapt to a new person in the house that they don't know? We may be so amazed and delighted to have found someone else to love who loves us that we are surprised when our children find it difficult to accept a new person in the house that they haven't chosen to be with.

It can take a long while for children to adjust to the fact that their parents have separated. The introduction of a new partner is often a real issue for the children, throwing them back into the same emotions, worries and feelings of guilt that they had at the time of the divorce.

In interviewing a friend for this book, I asked her what advantages she thought having a stepfather had brought her. Her mother had remarried when she was twelve. To my surprise she couldn't think of any. She could see that there were advantages for her mother, but not for her. I don't think it has to be this way. There are many successful families that include step-parents, and the way you handle it can make all the difference.

INTRODUCE THE NEW ADULT GRADUALLY

This is actually how not to introduce a new adult...

Beth's story

Beth was living most of the week with her dad, visiting her mum, Chris, most weekends. Everyone was used to the arrangement. Then one day, Beth phoned Chris midweek. "I know it's not your weekend, Mum, but do you mind if I come over anyway?" She was fifteen, and sounded upset. When she arrived she told her mother why. "Sharon's come to stay and Dad knows I don't like her." Sharon was about twenty at the time. She was a girlfriend who had previously been in the area but who had been working elsewhere for a couple of years. Beth hadn't got on with Sharon before and had talked about that with her dad at the time. Then one day, as Beth put it, Dad came to pick her up from school and Sharon was in the car. "Sharon's coming to stay for a while," he said. "Just until she gets things sorted out."

Beth was upset that she hadn't been warned, she hadn't been informed, and it hadn't been discussed with her, even though "Dad knew how I felt about her". Maybe her father thought there was nothing to discuss; Sharon was an old friend and parents do have friends to stay from time to time. But Beth didn't see it like that any more; she was older now and understood that Sharon wasn't "just a friend". It wasn't long before she and Sharon were bickering. So what was the problem? They had argued over Sharon chewing gum! What was the problem with that? Nothing in itself. But Beth and her younger brother were not allowed to chew bubblegum. Nor could they stay up late to watch horror films, have expensive bubble bath, or swear in the house. But Sharon could. The main problem seemed to be:

"Why is Dad allowing her these special favours that he won't allow me?"

As Beth explained why she was so upset, Chris began to realize that it wasn't so much the fact that Beth's father had a girlfriend – he was allowed girlfriends; after all, her parents were divorced – but that Beth was suddenly expected to live together as "family" with someone who had different habits, and with whom she did not particularly get on. "We had a set of rules we were all brought up with," Beth said, "and that's just gone out of the window."

The situation came to a head when they were all out one day on a family trip. Beth asked her dad, as teenagers do, if she could have some money for new jeans. "Shouldn't your mother pay for that?" replied her father. Beth was explaining how she'd asked Mum, but... when Sharon jumped in. "Why can't you get your mother to pay for it?" she asked. "After all, you live with your dad and she doesn't pay for anything else... if your mum cared about you..." Sharon went on to say exactly how she saw the situation.

"You can't speak about my mum like that," said Beth.

"I can do what I ******* well want!" replied Sharon.

And, in Beth's words, "Dad just stood there. He did nothing. He didn't intervene – he said nothing." Beth's dad didn't take her side in the argument and that to her felt like a major betrayal. "A very serious thing" were her actual words. Until then, her parents had always been on her side and defended her against accusations, or people swearing at her. Whatever was in her dad's mind at the time, Beth felt that he hadn't taken her side – he'd taken the side of this new woman. The following weekend Beth brought a lot more of her stuff than usual to her mother's house, and she didn't go back to her dad's on Monday. Instead, she asked Chris if she could stay until Sharon left.

Maybe if Sharon had been introduced more gradually, or if Beth's father had reassured Beth that he was on her side, she might not have left his house so suddenly. Maybe if Sharon had stayed out of the jeans argument things would never have come to a head that day. For Beth, it was definitely the catalyst to moving back to her mum's. The sudden introduction of a new woman into the house, even temporarily, without any preparation or discussion with her, was too much.

I know that introducing a new adult into the family does not have to be like this. Alex's story at the beginning of the book is one of the thousands of instances where a step-parent comes into the house and it is fine, but in his case there was a lot of introduction and preparation before it finally happened and that is what children (even older children) need. Relationships nowadays in the Western world are so fluid, they grow and change and become more or less committed without any outward sign to the world. Over the last five years, I have seen my son Richard's relationship with the lovely Renata go almost imperceptibly from friend, to girlfriend, to long-term girlfriend, to live-in girlfriend, to partner, to wife. When there are just two of you involved, things can take their course – or not – in a fluid way like that, but when there are children to consider, taking things slowly and being clear about your intentions at every stage really helps them adjust. It also helps if there is some form of clear commitment between the two adults before they actually move in together.

Polly's story

My colleague Polly divorced when her daughter Becka was only two years old. Becka lived with her mum and visited her dad – who lived in a different county – regularly throughout her childhood. Her father remarried when Becka was seven, and had two children whom Becka grew up with like cousins, sharing a room with the eldest girl when she visited. Fourteen years later, Polly met and fell in love with Paul, a widower, who himself had three children. Polly was worried about the effect her having a "boyfriend" would have on her teenage daughter, but Becka was pleased for her mum and encouraged her to go out with him. Polly and Paul kept their relationship outside of the home. The children of both families knew their parent was "going out" with someone and chatted with them if they were around, but Polly and Paul didn't stay over at each other's houses when the children were there. This couple really did take it slowly but they were conscious that there were six people affected by their decision, not just the two of them. Slowly the relationships among the wider family grew to the extent that Paul was around at Becka's eighteenth birthday and Polly was being asked to help with homework by Paul's younger daughters. The families were getting used to having new adults around.

After about two and a half years, when both families were quite used to days out with an extra adult, Becka suggested that the children all meet. So finally they all had a day out together. Suddenly that was one step too far. Although they'd taken it slowly, and even though Becka had suggested they all get together, she was really upset by it. Emotional scars can take a long time to heal and can surface when we least expect it. Polly and Becka talked and eventually Becka worked out what the problem was. It went back to the time her father had had his new family. As a young girl, she could only ever visit her father and his new family as they lived so far away. She loved her stepbrother and sister and got on with them, but always felt like the visitor. As she grew up she formed the impression that her father's family wasn't really hers. She was a welcome visitor there, but not able to be a full member of the family. However, she could always come home to her mum. So families and family outings were associated in her mind with a form of exclusion. Suddenly being with a family again brought back a lot of "I'm not really wanted here". It seemed now that Mum was getting a family that didn't include her, just as Dad had back then. She felt as if she had lost her dad and now she was losing her mum. Polly was lucky in that Becka was old enough to work out what was worrying her and articulate it.

The eldest of Paul's children, who had left home, was not happy about the new arrangement either. And here comes a dilemma. How far do you put your own happiness aside for the children? Where is the balance? In every case it will be different. Rushing into things without telling the children definitely upsets them and brings up all the old insecurities they may have had about parents, families, love and acceptance, but parents can't keep their lives on hold for ever either. Steering a happy middle course is not an easy thing.

When Paul and Polly finally got to the point of getting all the children together from both sides to announce that they wanted to get married, the children surprised them both. They listened to their explanations of why they wanted to get married and asked their questions and talked through possible living arrangements... but there was something missing. Finally one of the boys voiced it. They wanted to hear Paul and Polly express their love for each other, out loud, in front of them. So they did. Then everyone was somehow relieved, Polly says.

Becka and Polly moved to Paul's family home. Becka is at college now, but has a room of her own in the house, decorated to her taste. The last I heard, both Becka and Paul's daughter Kitty were insisting that Polly should have as big a wedding as possible and were happily taking her out to choose wedding and bridesmaid dresses.

PARENTS NEED TO STILL HAVE INDIVIDUAL TIME WITH THE CHILD

A new relationship can be all-absorbing. Your heart longs for your new love and you only want to spend time together. Love is the same at whatever age it hits you, and the delight you have in your new partner can make your children very jealous and resentful. Older children, however, can be quite relieved when a new love comes into your life, as you are so much happier and they feel less responsibility to look after you. Even so, they still want their share of your attention. When you all move in together, this becomes even more important.

Make sure the child knows that the step-parent has not taken the parent's love for the child. It felt like this for a boyfriend I had back in my youth. I could never understand why at sixteen he had such a hostile attitude to his dad. It turned out that his father was his stepdad and they had never made a great connection. His parents had separated when he was very young and his biological father had had no contact with him and took no financial responsibility for him. So he'd had his mother's full attention until he was ten. "Then along comes this man and takes her away from me," he said. His mum went on to have two daughters with her new husband, and while Ben loved his half-sisters and gets on well with them to this day, there was a disparity in the way they were treated. Neither the father nor the stepfather saw Ben as his financial responsibility. Ben was a very talented young man and wanted to become a lawyer, but his family was too well off to qualify for a loan or grant and neither of his relatively rich fathers would support him through university. In the end a wealthy, philanthropic couple from the local church paid for his law studies. It was an amazing and beautiful outcome for him and he practises as a lawyer today, but so much confusion and anger could have been avoided at the time had his father or stepfather taken financial responsibility for him.

TREAT ALL THE CHILDREN EQUALLY AND FAIRLY

It is important if a reconstituted family is to function as a family that all the children are treated equally. A family with a step-parent can work well. Sophie had five young children when her husband left her, and brought them up with considerable difficulty on her own for five or six years. She met Jack when her youngest was at nursery. With so many little ones it was very clear that if he married her, he would be gaining a whole family. Jack worked hard at his relationships with the children as well as Sophie and bought and renovated a large house they could all move into.

Initially they had decided five children was enough, but Jack had not had any children of his own and Sophie loved her large family, so they went for one more pregnancy, which turned out to be twins. So they were a family of seven children. They made a series of tiny rooms, little cubicles, with beds built halfway up the walls and desks or toy boxes underneath, so each child could have their own individual space, from teenager Izzy to the baby twins. There was a real feeling in the house that everyone was treated the same. So much so that the twins got quite upset when they grew up a bit because when the others had a weekend away visiting their dad, the twins wanted to go too.

Others don't experience such a generous attitude from their step-parents. Paula writes:

> *Issues began when my stepdad and Mum had more [children]. Total inequality. I and my full blood siblings were then shelved to second rate in terms of presents, general stuff, pocket money etc. Favouritism was definitely shown to the two youngest siblings from the remarriage. I can remember my maternal grandma commenting when I was 14 or so that she could understand my stepdad having favourites but my mother shouldn't, so it was clearly obvious to other family members too.*

All children have a very strong sense of fairness. It's the biggest cry I hear in the classroom, as friends compare their marks or consider their commendations. "You gave her four and I only got three. That's not fair!" It's so keenly felt. I'm just a teacher. How much more do they feel it if they perceive Mum or Dad to be unfair? As well as being a stepchild, Paula is now a step-parent and her experience has influenced the way she treats her stepchildren:

> *I married when the children were 11 and 14, my husband had joint custody. When our daughter was born, the children were 14 and 17 – they did and do adore her and the feeling is mutual. We tried very hard to treat all very fairly – and still do. Even though the older two have left home now and have their own families, we still spend the same on all three for Christmas and birthdays and try and give time accordingly. The older two and their families are over almost weekly for dinner and much advice is shared re houses, relationships parenting etc.*

Step-parents can have an amazingly positive influence on their stepchildren. In most divorces the parents are divorcing each other, not their children, but in a small minority of cases there are parents who have abandoned, abused or rejected their children. In addition there are those parents who have so many problems of their own, in terms of mental illness or addictions, that they are not able to give their children the parenting they would like. In such cases, to have another adult who cares for them and looks after them can be immensely affirming and life-changing for the child, as all foster and adoptive parents know.

Children know this as well and a significant few of the children I surveyed gave statements such as those given below when asked about the advantages of divorce or separation. These children are still in regular contact with their birth parents but sometimes they were relieved to have a new family and step-parent. Children may want a man around the house who is interested in them, a woman who will go shopping with them, or brothers and sisters they have never had. The survey frequently threw up these feelings. It is summed up in this comment "There's potential for new family members/ step-parents", which came in answer to the question "What advantages are there in divorce?"

MAKE SURE THEY KNOW YOU ARE NOT TRYING TO REPLACE THEIR FATHER/MOTHER

However good the step-parent is, they cannot replace the child's original father or mother, and most children do not want them to. Having a new step-parent does not have to cause tension once it becomes clear that the child is still going to see their birth parent, and as long as the step-parent does not try to take over a role they do not have. It helps the child if the step-parent can explain that their role is as an adult friend, not a substitute parent. It is a different sort of relationship, especially when the child already has good and ongoing contact with their birth mother or father. Even though the relationship with stepchildren is different, it can still be a good and fruitful relationship on both sides. As well as taking the time to build a relationship with your new spouse, it will also take time to build a friendly relationship with their children, to find out what they like and dislike doing, and what activities they would appreciate you being part of.

My story: Grown-up stepchildren

I was ten years on my own before I met the man who was eventually to become my second husband. We met at one of those annoying events where the leaders decide to play those mingling games where you meet people you are not familiar with. It was not love at first sight. I didn't really want to "hold hands in a circle", especially with a man I did not know.

My husband says of being a step-parent to my grown-up children that he sometimes feels like a spare part. There but not there; involved but not involved. All four of my children discuss their life decisions and issues with me and with their father. The extent to which they may include my husband in the conversation depends on their individual relationship with him, and the style and depth of his friendship with each of them is different. This is, of course, much easier when the children have left home and are only coming for occasional advice anyway, but when you actually do have day-to-day oversight and care of the children in your house, it is more difficult and may set up tensions that parents are not always aware of. Outwardly, a mother and a stepmother look the same. So do a father and a stepfather. They may both pay the children's bills, buy them presents on their birthdays, mop their tears when they cry, and worry about them. In some cases a stepmother or father may act more like a mother or father to the child than their original parent, but actually, even though it looks the same, the relationship is and always will be different. Primarily Mum will be Mum (whether she is a good mum or not) and a stepmum will always be a friend, even if her mothering skills are excellent. I think this is part of what Paula means when she says she finds Mother's Day difficult:

> *I've tried really hard to love the older two as my own and think I do – Mother's Day is one of the hardest days; there is no recognition of just how much sacrifice I've made at making these relationships work – their Mum just gets too jealous – being a stepmum is the hardest thing I have done and still do ... it's a really sacrificial role, especially with the mother still very much involved in their lives too. It's very much a behind the scenes role ... and yet if the youngest stepchild has been in trouble it is me she*

has come to for advice and help and was me who she
trusted to babysit first for her new-born daughter ...
but that can't be vocalized – it comes at too high a
price. Christmas and birthdays etc we haven't seen
the children on those actual days and that is hard –
they are with their Mum then and she puts too much
emotional pressure on the children (even now) if we
rock the boat by asking to see them on those days.

DEALING WITH THE ABSENT PARENT

Even if the child's parent has died, a step-parent can never replace the parent that is lost. How much more so when that parent is still alive and active in the child's life? As Paula points out, there is always the real mum or dad who has a claim on the children's time, love, energies and special moments. How you speak about them or relate to the stepchild's absent parent can have a profound effect on the child's relationship with you. What you say may be true, but children are very defensive of the parents they love, despite their faults, and are very sensitive to tension between the adults in their lives. Any criticism of their parent or arguments with them will throw the child into guilt for being (as they see it) the cause of upset in their family. They consider that you wouldn't be having the argument if they weren't there to maintain the connection with this person you don't like. Even in the cases where a child barely knows their absent parent and has formed a really good relationship with their step-parent, they may still want to meet their birth parent to help understand who they are.

As this book is about helping children through their parents' divorce and the ongoing consequences for them, I have not talked much about the effect on the parents themselves. I do know the pain divorce causes and the reasons why people divorce. I don't think people do it lightly, especially if they have children. If two people separate it is because of irreconcilable differences. The "irreconcilable" is important. Everyone I know who has divorced spent quite a time, sometimes many years, trying to find a way of reconciling their differences first. People find it hard to live with partners with addictions (alcohol, gambling, drugs) or who refuse to give up another sexual relationship, and they find it hard to live with bullying, mental illness or emotional, sexual, or physical abuse. In addition, it is very hard to continue the relationship when you have been deserted by your partner! Mediation services and organizations such as Relate find marriages can survive if both partners want them to, but if any one of the above is involved, it makes it very difficult. If there are two of the above present in a relationship, it is almost inevitable that the couple will separate.

If we accept that this is the case, then most divorced people will have very good reasons to be resentful or wary of their ex. So for most divorced parents, despite the grief of losing the person they loved, there is an element of relief that they don't have to live with the difficult behaviour. And so it is for some of the children. Even so, most children still want contact with both parents, no matter what they have done. For step-parents, this may be difficult to cope with. It is not always obvious from outside a relationship what is going on inside, but step-parents know the facts, and how much the person they love was hurt by their ex. Yet they still have to have some sort of contact with them because of the stepchildren.

The children know this. And so the loyalty bind they get into, even as adults, can be very difficult. Now there are three people they may upset, whatever they decide to do about their birthdays or Christmas. I know this is a common dilemma for many of us at major holiday times – whether to stay at home or go to Mother's or the in-laws this year – with all the attendant emotional pulls. In a reconstituted family, this problem is literally multiplied.

At primary school, my daughter was intrigued to find out that her best friend had *four* sets of grandmas and grandpas, as both sets of grandparents had divorced and remarried before she was born. I know one family that has solved this problem by cancelling Christmas in their house. They go away as a couple to somewhere non-Christmassy, which leaves their grown-up children free to divide Christmas around the rest of their family. Then, in February, when the weather is at its dullest in England, they throw a "winter party" and invite all the children and grandchildren when they won't have other pulls on their time. It's a creative solution. If a parent has to compromise with the other possibly more "difficult" parent over the children, then the step-parent has to compromise too. This can be hard when you are one stage removed and can possibly see more clearly the effect it is having on the family as a whole.

DISCIPLINE

Approaches to discipline and boundaries are discussed in Chapter 7 and apply to step-parents as well. The added complication for a step-parent is that their authority comes from the child's parent. As a rule of thumb it is wise to make sure you always back up what your partner has said in the matter, and see it through. Siding with the child against your partner should be avoided. For example:

"You can't have a biscuit – you know Mummy says no biscuits before dinner."

"But I *want* a biscuit and I want it *now!*"

"Fine, go on then. Just keep quiet about it!"

This may get you some peace in the short term but will ultimately undermine both your authority and your partner's. Formalizing a set of house rules may help everyone.

NEW BABIES

So you've taken it gently, explained you are just a friend to the children rather than a father or mother replacement, you haven't criticized the absent parent, you have built a new relationship with each child, you allow them regular space with their parent at home and have got used to sometimes feeling like a spare part while still treating everyone fairly... Then you announce the new baby is coming along and suddenly everything goes back to square one.

No one said being a family was easy. The Joseph Rowntree Foundation research concluded that "the more changes there are in the children's lives, the more problems they are likely to have".[1] Individually the changes that happen in a child's life might not seem that problematical, but taken together they can really add up. Take the hypothetical case of James. This story is entirely made up, but I haven't included anything particularly unusual or uncommon.

Imagine that James is born to loving parents aged twenty-two and twenty-five. When he's three, a new sister comes along (1) and he feels the normal jealousies and tries to hit her when Mum's not looking. Mum is stressed because she hadn't expected to have a family so soon and there are no jobs available for her skills that will fit round a family. But Dad finds work in another town with much higher pay and stays with a mate there during the week while the family stay in the area they know, where Mum's family and friends are around to help out (2). Infidelity is the commonest reason for divorce, so maybe Dad has found a new lady or Mum has enjoyed the visits of an old flame who's come to help out while Dad's not there. Whatever the reason, when he is six, James's parents divorce (3). James and his sister move out to a new smaller flat with Mum, and visit Dad in the holidays (4). Mum meanwhile gets a full-time job, leaving James and his sister with Grandma before and after school (5). When he's seven, Dad has a new baby and calls him David

James. Dad and Angie, his new partner, say James is always part of the family but James now feels superfluous when he goes to visit (6). When he's eleven, Mum remarries (7) and they move house again to live with his stepdad and new brothers aged nine and three (8). The new house means James goes to secondary school in a new area near where his stepdad lives and he misses his old friends (9). Two years later James is thirteen and another baby sister is born to his mum (10). At fourteen James moves to Dad's to get out of the chaos (11) and starts his GCSEs in a new school (12). My point? James has now had twelve major changes in the fourteen years of his life.

We all know that it is common for children to be jealous of new babies and the time and attention they need. I remember my eldest son's reaction when I came into the room to find him repeatedly hitting his baby brother on the head: "I not hitting him – I'm just blessing him *hard!*" (So much for taking them to church.)

Parenting is hard in all circumstances. My daughter and her partner say they feel so much more grown up than their peers now that they have a child. You do have to be so "adult" as a parent: more responsible, more organized, more committed to earning a living, less selfish and more aware of the needs and feelings of a range of other people. I don't think that being a parent as a divorcee or a step-parent is any worse, and it doesn't need any new sort of strategy from those that any parent would employ. It's just that the problems are sometimes more obvious in children who, like "James", have already had a lot of disruption in their lives. Because this change comes at the end of a long line of changes, it has more impact. It can bring up unresolved tensions or jealousies that the children might have felt over the divorce or the new step-parent, or their relationship with existing step-siblings. Talking about it, keeping them informed and involving all of them with the pregnancy and birth of their new half-brother or sister will effect a smoother transition.

Coming back to Paula, as a stepchild and a step-parent herself, she was conscious of the impact a new baby could have, and she took pains to involve the children in their new sister's life right from the beginning. She writes that when her daughter was born, the children – who were fourteen and seventeen – adored her:

> *We just told them... at 6 weeks as I was vomiting*
> *every morning – they loved being involved in the*
> *pregnancy – the 14 year old was doing a GCSE in*
> *child development and used me and her baby sister*
> *for several projects!*

One of my students went one step further and became birth partner to her mother. She then held her new half-sister the moment she was born.

If the new addition to the family brings up old unresolved problems, then it also presents an ideal time to talk about and deal with them. Involvement in the arrival of the new baby is an opportunity to cement family relationships and find out what it means to be this family together.

We like to think in our heads that the "norm" for a family is two children (a boy and a girl, of course) living with two parents, male and female, who married for love and live together all their lives. This is the norm for some – my own parents included – but for many, many people, "family" means single parent, stepfamilies, grandchildren brought up by grandparents, adoptive parents, foster parents, house-parents, travelling parents, council children's homes and probably more changes than we might like to have had. Families come in an almost infinite variety of forms. Usually, all children want is reassurance that their form of family is always going to be there for them, and that somewhere they are still accepted and wanted and loved.

NEW FAMILY IN SHORT

- Introduce the new parent gradually.

- Parents still need one-to-one time with their child.

- Make sure the child knows that the step-parent has not taken the parent's love for the child.

- Make sure they know that the step-parent is not trying to replace the child's own father/mother.

- Treat all children equally and fairly.

- Involve all children in the arrival of a new baby.

- Inform all children about changes in the household.

- Take care to speak about and relate to the child's absent parent civilly.

- In matters of discipline, always back the child's parent and follow what they do and say.

9

Changes
· · · · · · · · · · · ·

"It won't always be the same." (Rachel, 24)

One thing to realize in helping youngsters is that although six months, two years, five years or more may have passed, the issues have not. The child may be less tearful, less angry, less introverted and more adjusted as time passes but the loss of family as it was, and the loss of day-to-day contact with at least one parent and possibly siblings is huge. Like bereavement, it doesn't go away after a year or two. What's more, children, unlike adults, keep growing, physically, emotionally and mentally. A five-year-old has very different needs and problems from a ten-year-old, and a fifteen-year-old has different needs and problems again. For an adult, five years on from the split may mark a time of stability after the storm. Everything has changed, but now the new life is predictable again. For an adult, once you have the new job, new house and new partner or new single life, the patterns remain more or less the same. But a child is constantly changing, and each stage of maturity brings a new readjustment to the fact that their parents live apart.

Take something as simple as visiting the other parent at the weekend. This may be fine when you're five and excited by the attention and change of scene. Do you feel the same at fifteen, when you want to spend your free time with your mates?

Every divorce is different. People are unique individuals and circumstances vary so much. Even two families living in the same town, each with two working parents and two children of the same age, will find their arrangements and reactions very different. But whatever the arrangements made for the children initially, they will change.

Mary's story

When Mary's husband took their two sons away to live with him, she was devastated. She thought that he would come to his senses in a few weeks. She believed that he would at least see that the boys needed their mother, their little sister and their family home. She thought the boys, who were only six and eight, might be so upset they would insist on coming home. What she didn't know was that all this had been planned and thought through by her ex in some detail. It never occurred to her that he might have already investigated the legalities and found out what to say and how to say it to put himself in the best light. She didn't know that there was a way of accessing emergency housing benefit so that he and the boys were assisted by the state, and she had no idea that he had been subtly preparing the children. Mary had thought that it was a strength of their marriage that they had always shared the care of the children and the chores. At the time of the split, she had a full-time job and he had a part-time job so the children were used to their dad doing the school run, the shopping and cooking the meals.

After they had left, he carried on doing all the normal things in the normal way, decorated the children's new rooms for them in the way they wanted, and was generally a lot more settled than he had been before. But she felt she'd been thrown into a maelstrom of chaos and grief. In shock, she tried to catch up with all the things he had already thought through. It took a long time. When it finally dawned on her that he had gone, the boys were living with him and the family was irrevocably

split, she thought things would never change. But they did...
after some years, that is.

Mary told me, "If anyone had said to me back then, 'In two
years' time or in four years' time, the boys will be back living
with you and their sister,' I wouldn't have believed them. They
seemed so happy together with their dad. And I'm not sure it
would have helped me if I'd known. After all, I'd never been
apart from either of the boys for more than a few days. How
would I even be able to bear two years [of] living apart? It didn't
seem possible." But it did happen. The boys eventually decided,
as they got to the age of about ten, that they wanted to live with
their mum and sister again, and close to their friends.

There is so much rejection surrounding the break-up of a
long-term relationship. So any changes that the children might
want to make in the time they spend with either parent or the
home they want to base their current life in can be seen by
the parents as even more rejection, piled on top of the massive
hurt that is already there. Or it is seen as unfair influence by
the other person. Therefore any suggested changes may meet
with a strong emotional reaction from one or both parents, and
renewed rows and tension. The children are very conscious of
this and want to avoid upsetting either parent, but their wish
for change is often based on the way their life is changing and
not on a wish to reject either parent.

CHILDREN CHANGE

I used to hate it when my grandparents would say, "How
you've grown," when I saw them after a gap of a few months.
Yet children do keep growing and changing at a tremendous
rate, and with every milestone their needs change as well. A
great system for a three-year-old might not be the best for a
twelve-year-old. What the child wants will change too. When
you are five, being near the ballet class and the sweet shop may

be what you would like. At fifteen, being in the same town as your boyfriend and one street away from the youth club could have more appeal.

When they are babies, children often only see their visiting parent once a week and are taken back to sleep in their main home. At primary school age, though, it is common for children to spend weekends, long weekends and holidays with their other parent. Good forward planning and communication really helps here. Generally speaking, the children are capable at this age of enjoying longer stretches of time with their visiting parent and so it is likely that the initial arrangements will change. Whatever stage they were at when their parents split, the children continue to grow and change, so the arrangements made for them will change as well. It is helpful to the child if the adults in their life can anticipate these changes.

The most difficult time for separated families can be when the children become teenagers. Whatever their home circumstances, most teenagers want to spend time involved in their favourite pastime or with their friends. In one recent conversation in the staff canteen, mums were talking about supporting their sons at the football match, and the change that suddenly comes over them in their teens when they no longer want their parents jumping up and down delightedly when they've scored a goal. Congratulations and hugs and pride have suddenly got to be more circumspect, and their sons' concerns are suddenly for their girlfriends to be on the supporting line rather than their mums. (Shame their girlfriends don't drive and wash their kit.)

For parents who may already feel their time with their children is limited, this stage can come as quite a shock. Both my ex-husband and I found the whole system of "my weekend/your weekend" ceased to have much relevance when the children became teenagers, as we hardly saw any more of the children on "my" weekend than we did on "your" weekend. If it was Dad's weekend, the boys would yell "Bye" in the morning as they ran out to their father in his car and I wouldn't see them until Sunday night. If it was Mum's weekend, the boys would yell "Bye" in the morning as they ran out to meet their mates for a kick about (followed by hanging round the town, followed by lunch at Subway, followed by computer games at Doug's and a sleepover at Kevin's) and I *still* wouldn't see them again until Sunday night. I suppose if it was "my" weekend there was marginally more chance of seeing them over a meal. Their dad said the same as well. With four children, suddenly the whole weekend turned into a sort of complicated taxi service for us both, with pick-up points and venues changing at a moment's notice in a phone call. This can seem like rejection to separated parents, but really it is just the children's needs changing; the adults in their lives need to change with them.

At this age too they are much more likely to want to change the proportion of time they spend in each household. Initially, I was worried about the arrangements we'd made for seeing the children and I remember my solicitor commenting, "These things tend to find their own level." I didn't find this helpful at the time, but she was right. Michael, at sixteen, was already at the stage where his social life was more important than spending time with his family, and he was under a lot of pressure with exams as well. He wouldn't play "the weekend game", choosing instead to see his parents on his own terms and fitting them in around his Saturday job, schoolwork, girlfriend and mates. Richard, son number two, was fourteen at the time of the split, and for a couple of years did follow the arrangements made, but then decided that a more suitable arrangement for him would be a full week at his dad's and then a full week with me. As the girls became teenagers, their arrangements got more fluid as well. First Abigail began to stay for long weekends and to leave more and more of her things at my house. She finally decided to base herself with me, and visited her dad. A couple of years later, Rachel made the same move. In the end the boys were largely based at their dad's and the girls with me, a complete reversal of the first arrangement.

So it was that the flow went backwards and forwards and in it all there was an incredible sense of fairness too among the children. They tried hard to keep both of their parents happy. So my solicitor was right; it did all find its own level and it was not always what we expected.

Robert's story

Robert told me that when he was promoted to another part of the country, he and his wife decided their marriage was no longer working. She was not prepared to move with him and he was not prepared to give up his career prospects, so they agreed to part. They worked all the details out together and presented their case to the court. After two years of Robert being in his new job at the other end of the country, they received their decree nisi. Robert's daughter Sue was eight at that time and lived with her mother, keeping the security of her school and friends in the area. She visited her dad or he visited her at holiday times. Robert missed his daughter but never thought she would live with him again.

One day he came to ask me about schools in our area, with a look on his face of dazed confusion and delighted worry all at once. Sue's mother was at her wits' end, worried about her progress at school, and the wrong set of people she had got in with. She said she was finding Sue uncontrollable. All of a sudden, it had been decided that the best way out of the circumstances would be if Sue came to live with her father. So suddenly, at the age of twelve, it was all change. Sue did come to live with her dad, and went to a completely new school where, away from the influence of her old peer group and with the clear but fair boundaries her father set her, she blossomed into a well-balanced teenager. She lived with her dad until she went to college.

GETTING USED TO DIFFERENT HOMES BRINGS CHANGES

When two people live together, their lives merge and it is not always clear where the systems and atmosphere in a home originate. When parents separate and their households settle down, it becomes easier to see what each individual is really like in their habits and attitudes at home. When my own family split up, the children began to notice that Dad liked cooking. Mum cooked well, but Dad loved it and there was always good food there. (Yes, they now admit that as teenagers they sometimes did check out what was on each menu first before deciding where to spend the evening.) On the other hand, Mum liked gardening. Dad had a garden and planted flowers but the garden at Mum's was always full of colour and blooming all year round (more pleasant for sunbathing and "revising" in the summer).

I'm not talking about problems here, just differences. Some people's homes have regular routines and others are more relaxed about mealtimes and bedtimes. Some homes are noisy and crowded with lots of people, others are quiet with hardly any visitors. But what is peaceful for one child may be lonely and boring for another. What is stimulating and exciting for one child might be overwhelming for another. Even when the children are consulted and integrated into the decisions about their future, even when they choose and adults listen to their choices, they might find their choice was not as they had imagined. They might crave the order – or the freedom – that was in the other home. No one can really anticipate these things until it all pans out in real life. Depending on their characters, children might find that although they love both their parents, they just feel more at home in one house than the other.

I think it is these subtle differences that made so many of the pupils I surveyed write that one of the advantages of divorce was that you got two homes. Maybe it's good to have the chance to paint your room deepest black or vibrant pink at Dad's, even if it isn't allowed at Mum's. Or sleepovers at Mum's might be possible when they are not at Dad's. Mum's allergic to dogs but Dad has three. It's really clean at Dad's house, but you have to take your shoes off and can't eat in your room. You can eat where you like at Mum's; she doesn't mind if you get muddy footprints on the carpet, but it's hard to find a clean plate in the kitchen and the cat's often sick on the floor.

Good, regular access to two homes is seen as an advantage by many children. Maybe it's just practical; with Mum working so many evening shifts they actually feel safer being at Dad's, or Dad's house being further from their friends' homes means it's so much easier to carry on their social life if they are living with Mum. Mum's is convenient for primary school but Dad's house is right next to the secondary school.

LIFE CHANGES

None of us can predict the course life will take. Many circumstances largely out of our control can change the children's lives. As well as their parents meeting new partners, or new siblings arriving, there are dozens of other life-changing possibilities. Sudden accidents, illness or death can occur at any time in the close or wider family, as can promotion or redundancy at work. There might be a flowering of an exceptional talent in the child – music, football, dancing – or a sudden unexpected inheritance. Life is not always tidy or predictable. These changes may mean the child needs to base themselves more with the other parent at certain times.

Teenagers especially report that it helps them if they are allowed to make changes as their circumstances alter. Yet I know that these changes are often resisted by parents, grandparents and others, who feel the child is saying that they love the other side of their family more. Or maybe a parent objects because they disapprove of their ex-partner's lifestyle. What is "right" for the child will vary from one to another, and will probably change as circumstances change. To parents who feel they are not seeing enough of their children – or that they are taking on too much of the burden – I can say that in the future it will probably all change. To parents who have loved having their son or daughter with them all the time or who disapprove of their partner's way of upbringing, I'll say, "Don't hold on too tight." They are not rejecting you; it's that circumstances have changed. Holding them against their will causes them to fight harder or to descend into resentment. Allowing them to explore their relationship with their other parent more fully helps them to find out the truth for themselves. Their love for the other parent does not diminish their love for you.

ADULT CHILDREN ARE STILL YOUR CHILDREN

Children spend the majority of their lives, maybe up to fifty years if you are lucky, as your adult children. Even if children are unable to have contact with one of their parents when they are young, things often change when they become adults. Here are some stories of adult children who came to know their fathers later in life.

Lewis's story
Lewis was in his fifties when he spoke to me about his experience of his parents' divorce, so he was talking about something that happened about forty years ago. In those days it was taken for granted that mothers looked after the children and fathers provided for them. Therefore Lewis and his brother and sister continued to live with their mother while their father moved out, and yet he continued to support his ex-wife and children financially in the marital home. His mother left the children in no doubt as to where she thought the blame for the divorce lay, and discouraged the children from having contact

with their dad. Lewis's father's work led him to another town a good distance away and then all contact ceased. For years, the children did not see their father. However, Lewis said that even when they were very young, although they only ever got their mother's side of the story, they understood that what she was saying was only a version of the truth.

As they were growing up they would have liked to have had contact with their dad but they knew what their mother's reaction would be and the trouble it would cause. To keep the peace they held their peace. Sometimes our children have to show more patience and more wisdom than we do. Lewis says that as soon as they left home, the children each went out of their way to re-establish contact with their father. They had never forgotten him and they had never believed everything their mother had said. Our children are cannier than we give them credit for. It was a long wait for Lewis's dad, but he hadn't lost his children as he thought he had. Lewis did re-establish a good relationship with his father, which has lasted to this day.

Matilda's story

Tilly was only sixteen when she shocked her mother by saying she wanted to go and live with her dad in the USA. Her parents had split when she was a baby and she had barely met her father in all her life. She went to college in America and lived with her father during the course. At this stage in her life she had found a way of overcoming the huge distance between them. It was certainly a change for all concerned. It was very hard for her mother to lose her, but after completing her course, Tilly returned to the UK, having got to know her father.

Will's story

Will was twenty-one when he got a message on Facebook from his father. His parents had separated when he was a baby. His mum had left his dad and his nine-year-old brother in

Australia and taken him back to England. Will knew he had an older brother and a father in Australia but had never had any contact with them. He thinks his dad used to write when he was little but Mum didn't encourage the correspondence. After exchanging news, information and photos over Facebook for a year or more, Will decided to go out to Australia to meet the other side of the family. He was surprised at how much his brother remembered about him as a baby. He, of course, had no recollection of either of them. The last thing I heard, they were teaching him to surf. It is never too late to establish contact with children again if that's what both parties want. Will lost contact with half his family for twenty-one years, but he will now have a relationship with them for the rest of his life. Adult children are still your children.

CHANGES IN SHORT

- Children's needs change as they get older.

- Children might want to change the balance of time they spend with their other parents as they get older.

- Teenagers are usually preoccupied with their own lives first.

- We can't predict the changes life might bring.

- Coping with change can be a positive thing, making our children more resilient.

- Adult children are affected by their parents' divorce too.

10

Looking After the Parents

I am convinced that one of the best ways of making sure that children come through a divorce happily is to make sure the parents are looked after. Children only have one father and mother, and however adequate or inadequate they are, they are still, and always will be, the child's parents. Children will fare better if both their parents are settled and content, even if they can't be happy together.

WHEN IS THE DAMAGE TO THE RELATIONSHIP IRREPARABLE?

The first response of nearly anyone looking on as two people start towards a divorce is to try to help them mend the relationship before it's too late. Only this week it was marvellous to see the relief on the young face of one of my pastoral concerns as he confided in me, "Mum and Dad were arguing a lot and talking about divorce but they've sorted it out now." Emotionally, financially and in terms of the children's stability, it is much better if divorce or separation does not happen.

As I have been doing the research for this book, I have met a strong undercurrent of "Why can't they sort it out?" from very frustrated children, friends, grandparents, lawyers, family therapists and mediators, who are so conscious of the turmoil that divorce brings. Because I know first-hand the damage that divorce (or separation: more difficult as it is less clear-cut) brings, I don't welcome divorce. But I know it is not possible to mend every relationship and that it can be damaging to prolong the agony by trying to make two people stay together.

Divorced spouses can find the divorce transition even more difficult to get through when they are focused on the other person and getting them back. There comes a point when, as the lawyers say, the relationship has irretrievably broken down, and it is more helpful to accept the relationship is over and begin the process of starting a new phase in life. Sometimes this point is clearer to those looking on than to the friend or family member directly involved. So one way friends and family can help is to allow the divorcee to accept that the relationship has broken down and encourage them to move on, to look towards their future rather than living in the past. A refusal to let go prolongs the agony for all concerned, including the children. Support for the parent and help to face the future helps everyone.

EMOTIONAL HURT

All of the emotions that children may feel on the loss of their family are also being felt by their parents on the loss of their marriage and their partner. Add to that the difficulties of finance, housing and seeing the children, and you have a pair of exhausted parents. I have never known anything as draining and exhausting as the grief I felt at the loss of my family. The most stressful period at work just does not come close. It is really difficult just to keep going. Children don't really understand this. They expect their parents to be there for them, to carry on as normal, to provide for them and be with them and have fun like they always did. Often that is just not possible. Children are only children for a short time, so to make the divorce easier for your children, take time to look after yourself, physically and psychologically.

One of the best things you can do for your grandchildren is to give support and space to their parents. In looking after the parents, you make sure the children get what they need – the best possible contact with both parents in the circumstances. In Chapter 5 we looked at how just listening to the children caught up in divorce can be enormously helpful to them. In the same way, friends and family that will just listen to the ongoing storm of emotions in the parents are just as helpful for them and in addition help relieve the children of the burden of their parents' strong feelings.

HELPING WITH THE SHOCK

What surprised me about the "ordinary" divorce I went through was that the hurt was so bad while the circumstances were so normal. In most cases of separation and divorce, there is one partner who initiates the process and one who is taken by surprise. The emotional intensity of that surprise can be extreme. In any other circumstances, watching your children being driven off by a man in a white van or coming home to a locked house with an angry woman inside refusing you entry or access to your children would be a reason for calling out the emergency services. Yet every day these things happen as a "normal" initial move in a relationship breakdown.

To the partner who didn't realize this was coming, it doesn't feel normal at all. It feels as though there should be a national emergency going on. At this stage there is a real sense of unreality or a disassociation that comes over the shocked adult, often described as "like being in a nightmare". At this point, having friends and family who carry on as usual or a job and colleagues who continue to treat you as they always have can be very helpful, because it adds an element of stability to a world that otherwise appears to have gone crazy.

As the initial shock passes it leaves in its wake a profound loss of self-esteem in the parties concerned. Sometimes this is obvious. Sometimes it is covered up by brash or prickly behaviour. Here friends and family can rally round. Not by doing anything different but by continuing to do things the same way as always.

Empathy and acceptance are as important as practical support when you are emotionally bruised. If friends and family are acting as usual, inviting the divorcees over and including them in parties and outings, continuing to go with them to aerobics or the rugby club, it can feel amazingly supportive. Just to be accepted into a slice of ordinary life when everything at home is so extraordinary can be very reassuring and helpful.

PRACTICAL HELP

In every partnership, certain jobs usually gravitate to one partner or the other. One has responsibility for the house, the other for the cooking. When two adults separate, there are suddenly practical tasks all over their lives that their other half used to do. Gardening, cleaning, childcare, changing the beds (how do you get a double duvet cover on?), accounts, booking holidays, paying the bills on time, doing the washing, arranging direct debits, decorating, cooking, booking the car in for its MOT, getting the best price on insurance, doing the school run, putting furniture together, changing plugs, shopping... sometimes you don't even know what needs doing until it isn't done.

It is not unusual for adults to go half their lives without really knowing how to do some of these things, and for everyone there are bound to be things they are not up to speed with because their partner took responsibility for them for so many years. I know from personal experience that everything seems to take three times as long as it used to when there is no one to share it with. So one way to help the children is by taking some of these practical problems off the shoulders of their parents.

Sharing recipes that children will eat, recommending a reliable mechanic, offering to have the children for an evening or an hour or two after school, going round to help decorate; all these can help take some of the stress off a newly single parent.

MAKING SURE THE PARENTS HAVE THEIR LEGAL RIGHTS

It can be very difficult for people in a fracturing relationship to think of their ex-partner in a businesslike way. Taking such an attitude towards someone you have shared with in the most intimate way is a difficult psychological shift to make and can feel awful, especially if you didn't want the relationship to end. Somehow it confirms that it really *is* at an end. Yet it is a shift that will probably have to be made for the sake of the children. They need to know what arrangements are to be made, so these have to be decided. I know many women who have said, "I let him have the house/business/car just to get out of the awful situation." I have known parents who have left and gone away, thinking their children will be happier living securely with one parent rather than pulled between two.

It is not wrong to ask for a fair division of the assets held together, or to ask for financial contributions from the other partner in bringing up the children. Nor is it wrong for parents to want reasonable access to their children, even if these things may take a businesslike and legal turn which feels so wrong. In the end it is best for the children. Unless we are in the profession, few of us know how to advise our separated friends on this, as few of us know the current legislation. However, friends and family could suggest a local professional who would know. Legal advice is expensive, and some cynically say the only people who benefit from divorce are the lawyers, but a good family lawyer can help protect the rights of a separated partner against a difficult or manipulative spouse. Family lawyers know the ins and outs of the latest laws and are also aware of what arrangements other couples have made in similar circumstances. A good lawyer can make the whole legal process simpler and easier. In the UK the SFLA (Simple Free Law Advisor) website has some of the best advice I've found on the subject, as well as a directory of local family law solicitors and mediators (www.sfla.co.uk/).

If both the parents are in mutual agreement that they need to separate and are able to negotiate a reasonable agreement about the children with each other, then they can work it out between them. If it is not possible, however, for the parents to agree, a divorce mediator can provide a rational framework for discussion which can help both parents clear the emotional confusion and reach a workable agreement. Recommending a good lawyer or family mediator, or supporting them as they go to what can be emotionally difficult meetings, is one way in which you can help make the process easier, and ensure the children will have the best possible legal outcome.

HELPING YOURSELF

I remember being cross with my doctor when she told me I should make more time for myself. I was trying hard not to take any short cuts at work – people still expected me to do my job as well as I had before. I didn't want to take any less time with the children, as I already felt I didn't see them often enough. The home was taking twice as much looking after as it had before, as I took on all the tasks and duties that my husband had previously shared. Nothing at all got washed, picked up, cooked, tidied, painted or added up unless I did it. There was a steep learning curve as I took on the finances, insurances, bill paying and so on that was previously organized by my ex. On top of that there was the legal process to go through, *and* the grieving process. I felt as if I needed three lives just to exist. At least I could cut corners when it came to myself. I was wrong, though, and as I got more and more exhausted, I came to realize it. I was very lucky in the number of concerned people I had around me who said, "If there is anything I could do to help...?" But there is only so much that others can do and in the end you have to allow yourself to prioritize yourself. (If that doesn't sound too schizophrenic!)

Here are two things I found helpful in my journey to allowing time for myself. One was something I heard on the radio from Sister Frances Dominica, an Anglican Sister who founded the first children's hospice. In an interview, she was asked how she found the strength to be the support and companion she undoubtedly had been to so many people in such tragedy. She said she had learnt that in order to find time for others, she had to allow time for herself: "An hour a day, a day a week, a weekend a month, and a week a year." At first this sounded like a ridiculous amount of time to spend on myself, but after my breakdown I tried to take it more seriously.

I tried to make sure that after work, before I started my other job in looking after the house and the children, I had an hour to rest and recharge: reading, listening to music, walking or sleeping – whatever worked at the time. I tried, as I do today, to have one whole twenty-four-hour period without doing any housework or schoolwork. I began arranging things that I wanted to do on some of the weekends that the children weren't with me, such as seeing friends or joining local walking groups, and even though money was tight, I found ways of having a week's holiday each year by borrowing a kind friend's caravan, swapping houses with a friend or visiting family.

The other help I found was part of a staff training day on work/life balance. It was a way of helping you prioritize things in a busy life. The idea was you had two axes on a graph: one measured how important things were to you, and the other how much fun they were or how much you wanted to do something (see diagram below). I found it useful for helping to prioritize what was really important in my life, which was suddenly much busier than it had been.

Important/Enjoy	Important/Don't enjoy
Playing with the children	Going to work
Holiday	Doing the accounts
Visiting friends	Medical checks
Cooking	Washing-up

Not important/Enjoy	Not important/Don't enjoy
Watching soaps	Washing the car
Reading	Bringing work home
Surfing	Filing
Massage	Pruning the roses
	Cleaning children's rooms

The dotted box – things that are important and enjoyable

These are things to schedule into your life first. You enjoy doing them and there is no guilt in putting them first because they are important.

The dashed box – things that are important but not enjoyable

Whatever you put in this box is something you have to make time for. These things need a date in the diary or a system that makes them easier, so they can be done as quickly as possible. If you can't face these things, then there is a case for getting someone else to do them; employ a gardener or accountant or dog walker, buy yourself a dishwasher or get a cleaner. They are worth spending money on. If money's really tight, try swapping chores with a friend or family member. I knew neighbours once where No. 14 did the ironing for No.16 in exchange for No.16 doing No.14's accounts. This is also the box to consult when friends and family ask, "Is there anything I can do?" They could babysit the children while you go for your check-up, they could make going to work easier by doing the school run. They could pick your kids up from football training, as well as theirs. When you have friends round and they say, "Can I help with the washing-up?" don't say no.

The dotted shaded box – things that are enjoyable but not important

Whatever time's left over, fill it with things in this box – not so important but enjoyable. Make time for the things you do like, not the things you don't. With life changing so much, there might be the opportunity to start new things or reintroduce the things you enjoy into your life. It could be as simple as watching what you want on the television, or as challenging as starting a new sport or a degree course.

The dashed shaded box – things that are not important or enjoyable

In this box are things you don't have to worry about. You don't enjoy doing them and they are not important, so don't do them. These things are expendable. Leave the roses to look after themselves, give the children responsibility for the care of their own rooms, wait for the rain to wash the car for you and leave that extra work where it belongs – at work. It's not a priority at the moment.

TAKING CONTROL OF THE FINANCES

In a divorce or separation, most people's financial situation will change and it isn't usually for the better. You may find yourself running a household on one income rather than two, or you may find yourself dependent on your ex-partner's contributions which are sometimes sporadic. It is difficult with everything else going on for a divorcing parent to take a real honest look at the finances and budget, especially if this is something their partner always took responsibility for. Even if they are used to it, there will be a whole new set of budgeting requirements. In this age of paperless bank transfers and credit cards, many of us simply don't know how much we are spending each week on food, petrol or entertainment. When you actually write down realistically the amounts you are spending on utilities, rent or mortgage, food and petrol it can be overwhelming, but getting it all down on paper helps get it into perspective.

It also lessens the fear of not being able to cope. Even if you have been left with considerable debt there are ways of getting it under control. A good first step is to transfer all your credit cards and store cards to one card so that you have a clear idea of how much needs to be paid off each month. It might be a shock when you see the figure but it does show you what needs to be done. If, like a close friend of mine, you have been left with over £30,000 of your wife's debts and no job, you may need more serious advice and guidance. There are many free debt advisory services that can help you manage debt, even if it seems impossible to deal with. In the UK, the Citizens Advice Bureau and the directgov website[1] will give you details of free debt advisory services, and Christians Against Poverty is a free charity available to all, whether churchgoers or not, that is dedicated to helping people manage their debt (see www.capuk.org). My friend took advice from one such organization and is now debt free.

The CAB, as well as most banks and unions, have a budgeting pro forma which will detail the amazingly long list of categories that most people need to spend their money on. These budgeting planners can be really useful as they list things you may not immediately consider. It is frightening (it was to me) to look honestly at what goes out every month, but having a realistic idea gives authority to you and security to the children when it comes to what they actually need and what the family can afford. Whatever your ex-partner does or doesn't do, it will really help the children if you take control of your household finances. Getting to grips with the realities of your new financial situation, or helping a parent to do that, disperses the fear and worry and helps improve the atmosphere in the family home.

Financial planning needs to be long term as well as short term. Divorce can seriously affect the pension you will have when you retire and can affect your earning potential, because it becomes more important to fit work around shared responsibilities for the children. To have a clear head on this while you are in the middle of emotional turmoil is very helpful. When I was at a loss to know what to do, I really appreciated the hours my mum spent listening to me on the phone, but I also really appreciated the clear thinking and simple explanations that my dad gave me on financial matters.

PROFESSIONAL HELP

We have talked about professional legal help, but doctors have a range of options that they too can use to help parents who are in the turmoil of a divorce. Statistics tell us that at least one in three people will have some sort of mental health problems at least once during their life. To be depressed when you lose people you love is an entirely normal and natural reaction, and yet I think we still feel unable to ask for professional help for sadness or depression, even though we would not think twice about going to the doctor for antibiotics for a throat infection or calling an ambulance if we broke a leg.

If you would take aspirin for a headache, then why not take a sleeping pill for a disturbed night? When you wanted to lose weight, did you find it easier in a support group? Maybe a support group would help you adjust to the loss of your partner. If you would do a course of physiotherapy to restore strength to a broken limb, than why not sign up for a course of counselling sessions to help restore strength to faltering emotions? If you've ever been on a course to help build a skill for your work and your firm, then why not take a life skills course to help build your own personal resources in facing a new future? If you took a minor complaint to the doctor – a palpitation, maybe – and found it masked a more serious complaint, would you refuse the doctor's advice to see a heart specialist or brain consultant? There is no shame in finding that the normal depression of a relationship break-up is also masking, as it sometimes can, a deeper problem from earlier in your life. A consultant psychiatrist transformed the life of a friend of mine by diagnosing an unrecognized bi-polar disorder when she was fifty; her only regret was that she had not seen a specialist earlier. Others, through the professional help of psychiatric workers, finally come to terms with long buried issues of violence and abuse from their earlier life.

Every day people find their hurts healed and their recovery speeded up by the help of professional people, and the same is true of emotional and mental hurt as well. Lives are being transformed by skilled help, and I for one am grateful to both my doctor and my counsellor for their input in getting me through one of the worst times of my life.

There is a direct correlation between the way the parents adjust to the divorce and the way their children adjust. Looking after yourself if you are separated, or looking after your separated friends, is an efficient way of helping the children survive separation and divorce. The healthier and happier the parents can be in their lives apart, the better their children will adjust to the new way of being family.

LOOKING AFTER THE PARENTS IN SHORT

- Listen to them.
- Try to be as normal as possible.
- Offer financial advice.
- Offer practical help.
- Encourage them to take professional advice.
- Support if medical or counselling help is needed.
- Offer to look after the children to give them extra time.

Postscript

· · · · · · · · · · · · · ·

I hope that some of the stories and suggestions in this book have helped. Not everything is going to be applicable to your situation. Maybe something here will help you to help the children who concern you, whether they are your own children or your friends', your grandchildren or your pupils who are struggling with their parents' divorce.

It is now over fifteen years since my own divorce. I worried most about my children, but they have all adjusted well and manage to stay on good terms with both their parents. I am close to my girls as well as my boys. They all have good jobs and, even more importantly, good relationships. Two of my four children are getting married this year and that is one thing I wondered if they would ever do.

We have all found different ways of relating to each other, and although I think they might have preferred the family of their early childhood to have continued, everyone knows that they are still our children, that we both love them, and that we are still their mum and dad.

Booklist

· · · · · · · · · · ·

Gary Chapman, *The 5 Love Languages*, Chicago, IL: Northfield Publishing, 2010.

Gary Chapman and Ross Campbell, *The 5 Love Languages of Children*, Chicago, IL: Northfield Publishing, 2005.

Gary Chapman and Jennifer Thomas, *When Sorry Isn't Enough*, Chicago, IL: Northfield Publishing, 2013.

Jennifer Croly, *Missing Being Mrs*, Oxford: Monarch, 2004.

Adele Faber and Elaine Mazlish, *How to Talk So Kids Will Listen & Listen So Kids Will Talk*, London: Piccadilly Press, 2013.

Daniel Goleman, *Emotional Intelligence*, London: Bloomsbury, 1996.

Joan Halifax, *Being with Dying*, Boston, MA: Shambhala Publications, 2009.

Useful Websites

UNITED KINGDOM

Joseph Rowntree Foundation
www.jrf.org.uk

Kathleen O'Connell Corcoran's work is on
www.mediate.com

Simple Free Law Advisor
www.sfla.co.uk

For fathers' issues
www.dad.info

Children's health and divorce
www.netdoctor.co.uk/health_advice/facts/divorce.htm

All parenting issues
www.supernanny.co.uk

Children and mental health
www.rcpsych.ac.uk

Citizen's Advice Bureau
www.citizensadvice.org.uk/index/sitehelp/breaking_up_is_
never_easy

ChildLine
www.childline.org.uk

Legal aid
https://www.gov.uk/browse/births-deaths-marriages/marriage-
divorce

AUSTRALIA

Government advice
www.familyrelationships.gov.au/BrochuresandPublications
australia.gov.au/life-events/relationships/getting-divorced

Information on Family Law Courts
www.familylawcourts.gov.au/wps/wcm/connect/FLC/Home/
Children%27s+Matters/Children+and+separation/

Early Childhood Australia
www.earlychildhoodaustralia.org.au/feelings_and_behaviours/
managing_grief-loss-change/separation_and_divorce.html

Kid's Helpline
www.kidshelp.com.au/teens/get-info/hot-topics/separation-
and-divorce.php

Raising Children
raisingchildren.net.au/articles/coparenting.html

Parent Line
www.parentline.org.au

NEW ZEALAND

Government services
www.familyservices.govt.nz/my-family/raising-children/children
-and-divorce.html

Online divorce service
www.divorceme.co.nz

Divorce help
www.divorcehelp.co.nz

Relationship issues
www.relationshipsaotearoa.org.nz

Family issues
www.kiwifamilies.co.nz

Citizens Advice Bureau
ww.cab.org.nz/vat/fp/r/Pages/Separationanddissolutionofmarriage

Babies and children
www.plunket.org.nz/your-child/welcome-to-parenting/parenting/
parenting-apart/

Parenting help
www.theparentingplace.com

(All websites accessed 8 July 2013)

Endnotes

· · · · · · · · · · · · ·

Introduction

1. Jennifer Croly, *Missing Being Mrs*, Oxford: Monarch, 2004.

Chapter 2

1. Sir Nicholas Wall made these comments in a speech to the charity Families need Fathers. See
http://www.bbc.co.uk/news/education-11380470 (accessed 10 May 2013).

2. See http://www.mediate.com/articles/koc.cfm (accessed 10 May 2013).

3. See http://www.jrf.org.uk/publications/divorce-and-separation-outcomes-children (accessed 10 May 2013).

4. See http://www.dad.info/separation/children-of-separation-and-divorce-surviving-and-thriving-what-makes-the-difference/ (accessed 10 May 2013).

5. Adele Faber and Elaine Mazlish, *How to Talk So Kids Will Listen & Listen So Kids Will Talk*, London: Piccadilly Press, 2013.

Chapter 3

1. F. Mavis Hetherington and John Kelly, *For Better or for Worse: Divorce Reconsidered*, London: W. W. Norton and Co., 2002.

Chapter 4

1. See http://www.bbc.co.uk/news/education-11380470 (accessed 14 May 2013).

Chapter 5

1. Joan Halifax, *Being with Dying*, Boston, MA: Shambhala Publications, 2009.

2. F. Mavis Hetherington and John Kelly, *For Better or for Worse: Divorce Reconsidered*, London: W. W. Norton and Co., 2002.

Chapter 6

1. Gary Chapman, *The 5 Love Languages*, Chicago, IL: Northfield Publishing, 2010; Gary Chapman and Ross Campbell, *The 5 Love Languages of Children*, Chicago, IL: Northfield Publishing, 2012.

2. Gary Chapman and Jennifer Thomas, *When Sorry Isn't Enough*, Northfield Publishing, 2013.

Chapter 7

1. Adele Faber and Elaine Mazlish, *How to Talk So Kids Will Listen & Listen So Kids Will Talk*, London: Piccadilly Press, 2013.

Chapter 8

1. See www.jrf.org.uk (accessed 10 May 2013).

Chapter 10

1. www.gov.uk/options-for-paying-off-your-debts/overview (accessed 10 May 2013); http://www.nidirect.gov.uk/dealing-with-debt-problems-a-guide (accessed 10 May 2013).